Overcoming Student Apathy

Motivating Students for Academic Success

Jeff C. Marshall

Published in the United States of America
by Rowman & Littlefield Education
A Division of Rowman & Littlefield Publishers, Inc.
A wholly owned subsidiary of The Rowman & Littlefield Publishing Group, Inc.
4501 Forbes Boulevard, Suite 200, Lanham, Maryland 20706
www.rowmaneducation.com

Estover Road
Plymouth PL6 7PY
United Kingdom

British Library Cataloguing in Publication Information Available

Library of Congress Cataloging-in-Publication Data

Marshall, Jeff C., 1965–
  Overcoming student apathy : motivating students for academic success /
Jeff C. Marshall.
    p. cm.
  ISBN-13: 978-1-57886-852-0 (cloth : alk. paper)
  ISBN-10: 1-57886-852-1 (cloth : alk. paper)
  ISBN-13: 978-1-57886-853-7 (pbk. : alk. paper)
  ISBN-10: 1-57886-853-X (pbk. : alk. paper)
  ISBN-13: 978-1-57886-887-2 (electronic)
  ISBN-10: 1-57886-887-4 (electronic)
  1. Motivation in education. 2. Academic achievement. I. Title.
  LB1065.M336 2008
  370.15'4—dc22   2008017658

∞™ The paper used in this publication meets the minimum requirements of
American National Standard for Information Sciences—Permanence of
Paper for Printed Library Materials, ANSI/NISO Z39.48-1992.
Manufactured in the United States of America.

Contents

Acknowledgments   v

Introduction   1

1   The Rebel   11

2   The Socialite   27

3   The Misfit   43

4   The Overachiever   57

5   The Player   73

6   The Overwhelmed   87

7   The Downtrodden   99

8   The Invisible   115

9   Conclusion   127

About the Authors   133

Acknowledgments

My continued desire to learn, explore, and discover is largely inspired by my children, Anna and Bennett, who have an insatiable thirst for knowledge regarding the world around them. The wonder that I see in their eyes provides an ongoing reminder to me as an educator that no matter how apathetic a person seems on the exterior, there lies a vibrant mind that seeks to understand the complexities and interworkings of the world around us.

To my wife, Wendy, I give great thanks as she continually encourages me to grow and improve.

My former students, friends, and colleagues have challenged and continue to challenge me to excel each and every day. It is through the honest critique of my work as I teach, write, and communicate that I continue to learn new ways to improve my skills and abilities. Specifically, the students and faculty at Clemson University, Butler University, Indiana University, and Putnam City Schools have taught me so much about myself and about how to be a better educator.

Finally, it is with sincere thanks and immense appreciation that I thank Dina Bailey, Brian Dunn, Emily Laszewski, Abigail Parker-Kindelsperger, and Alicia Smith-Noneman, who have provided insightful feedback and fantastic written contributions. Their knowledge and understanding of teachers and students provided a vivid depiction of teaching and learning that all should be able to appreciate and relate to. It was, in part, the questions that they raised as pre-service teachers four years prior that formed the impetus for this book. Thanks for seeing this through to fruition.

Introduction

This book presupposes that all educators essentially share the same goal—positively affecting the minds and lives of *all* their students. This common goal, despite differences in school size and location, teaching styles, administrative structure, and resources available, unites educators in a collective struggle. Upon entering the profession of teaching, we set out to change lives and to help the world.

We were willing to do anything for our students, and assumed students intuitively share the same enthusiasm about the world around us. In many cases, this enthusiastic beginning, labeled as idealistic by some, clashed with reticence and apathy shown by many of our students. This book seeks to spark discussion, reflection, and action among educators on the real issues educators face every day. The ideas and potential solutions presented hope to inspire new ways of succeeding with the various types of student apathy that are seen in your classroom.

That being said, welcome to Roosevelt High. Though its size, the names of the students, and the attributes of the teachers likely differ from your school, the problems evidenced, joys celebrated, and general personality types seen will likely be quite familiar. The characters and scenarios will hopefully remind you of certain students, teachers, and situations that you currently encounter. Our tendency to make excuses for why certain students are not succeeding in school avoids going beyond the problem in order to seek viable solutions.

We hope the strategies in this book will allow educators to work smarter, not harder when encountering challenging situations. Additionally, we hope educators will see a bit of themselves in the teachers illustrated in this book. To win the battle against apathy in our schools, we must confront the challenges before us—not avoid them.

The school bell rings, signaling the beginning of a new day. The students filter in and assume their roles; teachers scurry around making last-minute preparations; administrators and security officers walk the hallways, encouraging straggling students to proceed to class; secretaries at the front desk fill out passes for students who need to leave school early. As the tardy bell rings, the halls that were cluttered with students moments before are now littered with random assignments and tattered papers. The classrooms are now filled with the students who *opted* to attend class today.

Classroom doors close, initiating the daily routine, but critical differences exist within the individual classrooms. The events and outcomes achieved in each classroom are unique even when the curriculum is departmentally controlled. As the bell rings to dismiss class, students leave with differing experiences.

Some are excited because they live for the next seven minutes called passing period—a seeming parole; others leave with wrinkled sleeves imprinted on their faces because they intentionally or unintentionally slept through class; others exit feeling dejected because of failure, yet again, on an assignment, quiz, or test; others saunter out knowing they are "winning the game" by having an A or B in the course; and a few leave with the excitement of a new discovery, a clearer understanding, or a sense of mastery regarding the day's lesson. The discussions sparked by this book promote more of the latter experience—developing satisfying learning experiences filled with hope, excitement, challenge, and, in the end, a sense of achievement.

Within the walls of our classrooms sits a vast array of talented students. For many, these talents are celebrated and applauded; yet, for far too many students these talents remain hidden, or worse, go untapped and undeveloped. The lucky ones, whose talents are recognized, become the heroes of our classrooms, schools, districts, and communities. These heroes and heroines are the ones whose work is lauded as exemplar for other students to follow. They are the ones who demonstrate for school board members and superintendents the model of excellence. They are the ones who get the awards, accolades, and scholarships.

Indeed, we need to celebrate the accomplishments of these students and encourage the continuation of their greatness, but this book focuses on bringing others to a similar tier of success. Central to this book are the antiheroes and the invisible students—the disenfranchised, downtrodden, and demoralized who permeate our classrooms and schools.

We are all familiar with the character archetypes that fill the pages of literature (such as the hero, the scapegoat, and the villain), but our middle school and high school classrooms are filled with their own unique set of archetypes. Successful hero and heroine archetypes (such as the valedictorian, the scholar, the thespian, and so on) are deliberately omitted here, replaced instead by the antiheroes seen in our schools.

The goal is to transform the unsuccessful and outcast students into individuals filled with hope that yearn for success. Much like a snake shedding its old useless skin, the term *antihero* seems more visually fitting than does its synonym *antagonist*. Semantics maybe, but the potential for success resides in all of us. We, as educators, must find ways to unravel this often complex cocoon—thus allowing the anti*hero* to be transformed into someone who possesses the qualities of the hero. The difficulty arises when we have run out of ideas and options for solving the challenges. Possibly this book will refresh your vision for how to better touch the lives of *all* students.

The narration, constructed for each antihero, sheds light on our understandings and misunderstandings associated with our middle school and high school students. The challenge is to assure that the value, abilities, and accomplishments of *all* students are recognized and celebrated.

We've all heard it in the teacher's lounge, and many of us truly believe it: "I am doing everything I can." "How can I acknowledge success when a student refuses to work?" "With all the push for success on high-stakes tests, there is no time to do anything else." "I am tired of feeling like I'm communicating with a brick wall."

Indeed, the current educational system is fraught with many challenges, but we must probe deeper. Until we truly understand how to unlock the potential within each student, success will be marginal. Furthermore, if the educational system remains constant, it will continue in the current quagmire where one-third of our students succeed, one-third *just make it* through school, and one-third drop out. Yes, even the best baseball players only succeed one out of three times at bat, but these odds cannot be the standard that we tolerate in our classrooms. As schools become more diverse and evolve in our ever-changing world, our approaches must continually adjust to meet the new and unique needs of *all* our learners.

Perhaps the greatest challenge for secondary-level educators, both the experienced and the neophyte, is to find ways to inspire and motivate students to engage in meaningful learning beyond just trivial restatements of basic content. This challenge becomes greater in underprivileged, largely minority settings where apathy is extremely pronounced. Apathy, although more prevalent in some settings than others, has become part of all schools in some form or another.

Eight different forms of apathy are presented in this book. Accompanying each of the eight narratives are strategies, ideas, and discussion questions to provide teachers and administrators a way to begin confronting the challenges of working with students who exhibit similar archetypal behaviors. Although the strategies should assist all teachers, they are meant to be merely a beginning. Ultimately, success comes when teachers work through the challenges and solutions together. The strategies highlight common challenges experienced by all teachers coupled with proactive ways to reduce the likelihood of the challenge interfering with future learning.

This book individually confronts each of the eight antihero archetypes evidenced in our classrooms. Each character is a compilation of various real students who fit the specific archetype. Each is explored from multiple perspectives: the student's, the teachers', and the often complex shared interpersonal interaction between the student and teacher.

For teachers resisting the temptation of mediocrity and complacency, this book is for you. The continuum of complacency is flanked by two dichotomous extremes. One extreme buys into the conscious or sub-conscious fallacy that some students succeed through hard work while the rest simply do not care, are unmotivated, and/or are just uneduca-ble. The other extreme feels successful with all students and feels no need to develop further as a teaching professional.

Regardless of the type of complacency, any tendency to give up on a student has tragic implications and must be vigorously fought. Who is willing to tell a parent that his or her child is uneducable? Absurd, you say? Many of us do this subconsciously when we turn our backs on the possible success of a student—particularly when success is not immediate.

The changes necessary for us as teachers often are small, but realize: small changes can have a large impact on the lives of your students and the quality of their learning. We all can afford to grow in understanding how to maximally impact our students.

The term *apathy* is most often used in schools to categorize all that plagues our classes. In its broadest sense, apathy robs our classes of the energy, passion, and enthusiasm that we aspire to create with our students each fall. Even many of our successful, bright students are recalcitrant to-ward learning and resist getting involved unless it is grade dependent. The terms used to characterize our apathetic students include *zombies*, *dead-beats*, *underachievers*, *uninterested*, *unengaged*, *dropouts*, and *losers*. Two things remain clear as we work with students who evidence the char-acteristics of apathy in our classes.

First, apathy is generally situational—not a chronic condition of one's life. Just watch the seemingly comatose spring to life as they jet past the classroom threshold after the dismissal bell rings; watch the vibrance that abounds in students as they pull out of the school parking lots in their cars filled with friends; watch teens in the malls or at neighborhood parks—life abounds with laughter, music, and verve. For these students, are the doldrums experienced within the classroom walls a necessary evil on the road to becoming a productive, educated citizen? I hope not.

Second, and most relevant for this conversation, is the realization that apathy is typically a manifestation of a deeper issue. We have all heard or been guilty of saying something to the effect of "Those kids just don't care." Yet, until we understand the root cause(s) of the apathy, a solution will elude us. This book considers eight faces (archetypes) of apathy. Each of the highlighted student characters within this book is representative of one of the eight different archetypes that teachers see on a daily basis. We should all be able to substitute the names of the characters in this book with the names of our own students.

Even though the characters illustrated within this book represent discrete archetypical issues (e.g., anger), reality tells us that each of our students is an amalgamation of infinite possible combinations. Despite this seeming tendency to oversimplify personalities, the characters provide a real starting point for discussions among teachers and administrators. Several guiding questions, interspersed throughout each chapter, help to initiate conversations regarding how to succeed with each apathy archetype.

The focus of this book arose from questions posed by student teachers as they grappled with apathy issues during their sixteen-week student-teaching experience. Five of these students—Dina Bailey, Brian Dunn, Emily Laszewski, Abigail Parker-Kindelsperger, and Alicia Smith-Noneman—continued the discussion beyond the classroom and helped develop the narratives for each of the featured archetypes. Although the more experienced cooperating mentors were more adept at organizational techniques, graphic organizers, assessment techniques, and grading, most all still grappled with the same questions. The questions that challenge teachers and serve to frame the discussions in this book include:

- How do you teach students that don't care about grades?
- Is the expectation that *all* students can and will learn reasonable and possible, or is it too idealistic?
- Do teachers expect failure from some students?

- How do you teach angry students (anger that originates inside and outside the learning environment)?
- How do you work with students who self-sabotage (won't accept success)?
- How do you work with students who *appear* lazy or unmotivated?
- How do you effectively engage those who are different from you (culturally, physically, socioeconomically)?
- How far should a teacher go to provide students with engaging, meaningful learning opportunities?
- How do you set high expectations and hold students accountable when they don't want to take any responsibility?
- How do you rescue individual students while still progressing as a class?

Each chapter follows a parallel format that includes: a brief introduction of the actual character representing the archetype, a narrative of the student interacting within the school setting, some strategies for working with these students, and some questions to help continue the conversation. The narratives are all written from the *fly-on-the-wall* perspective, where the observer sees the objective worldview perspective of both the student and teacher. Since perception is often considered reality, it is vital that we, as educators, understand how various archetypes perceive their educational world. Perhaps, by pausing and rewinding the tape to the earlier years of development, we can begin to see how the current conditions developed.

Studying the world of children is an amazing thing. A twenty-one-month-old demonstrates an unquenchable thirst for language. Kindergartners are fascinated and intrigued as they play and explore. First and second graders are naturally curious about the world around them as they ask such things as "Why does a worm wiggle?" Then, somewhere between third and sixth grade, students begin to clearly differentiate between schooling and learning. From then on, the *game of school* is in session.

The problem with this game is that no one really wins. We don't feel satisfied with the accomplishments of our students, and our students perceive no real value in the majority of classroom experiences from seven in the morning until three in the afternoon, five days a week. Einstein aptly contended, "It is, in fact, nothing short of a miracle that the modern methods of instruction have not entirely strangled the holy curiosity of inquiry." Is there a viable solution to this seeming quagmire of steeped apathy, low motivation, and minimal engagement? Yes. And that is what this book addresses.

The first chapter begins early in the first quarter of the school year with Aaron Rutledge, the Rebel, who typifies students that enter our classes with anger issues. Students like Aaron quickly get labeled as troublemakers when in fact their inappropriate behaviors are often misguided pleas for help. While it is unreasonable to think we can totally eradicate anger from our students, it is possible to improve communication skills and reduce the ire that inhibits success.

Next, Tina Hodges's constant need for social interaction results in a classroom conflict. Pleasant, easily distracted, and highly interactive are typical descriptors for Socialites like Tina. Integrating the need for social interactions with academic assignments helps to engage Socialites in a classroom setting.

Katherine Sweetbriar, the Misfit, emerges near the end of the first grading period and provides a unique look into the worldview of those who are cast aside either by choice or by pressure from social norms. Katherine exemplifies students that do not seem to fit the norm by erecting defenses to protect herself.

David Sanchez, the Overachiever, illustrates what is arguably the most commonly seen form of apathy. David gets so absorbed in the grade that he misses the key—learning. Success comes when teachers get the Overachiever like David to step beyond the *game of school* and assume more active involvement in the pursuit of knowledge, inquiry, and understanding.

Nearing the end of the second grading period, J. B. Harris, the Player, enters the story. His passion for sports keeps him in school, but school then becomes a series of hurdles that must be overcome to allow him to pursue his greatest passion, sports. Teachers can help by trying to broaden the intellectual horizons of students like J. B. and by making explicit connections to areas of passion.

Emi Choi illustrates the archetype of the Overwhelmed. Either because of poor planning or because she processes information differently, Emi reminds us as educators of the importance of clarity in exemplary classrooms. Specifically, students need to learn how to deconstruct major assignments into attainable fragments. Otherwise, students such as Emi become overloaded and lost when they become singularly transfixed on the bigger picture or final goal.

Nearing the end of the third nine weeks, Ivory Hill has given up after repeated encounters with failure. Downtroddens like Ivory quickly realize that after numerous low performances, achievement and success are not expected. Rebuilding low self-esteem can be accomplished through progressively scaffolding successes.

How appropriate that John White, the Invisible, would be left until the end. John fits so well into the norm that he rarely attracts attention for any reason. This individual may marginally succeed or find out at the very end that he just missed the minimum to succeed. The quietness of Invisibles like John is often interpreted as understanding, when in fact they may not know how to frame the questions to get the needed help. Or they may just seek to hide because of their lack of understanding.

As teachers we want to succeed with *all* our students, but maybe looking at our students as a conglomerate is part of the problem. It is when we begin to understand the complexities, desires, and interests of *each* student that we begin to succeed with all. The challenge becomes how to address the uniqueness of each student while still facilitating the learning of a large group.

CHAPTER 1

The Rebel
September 23

Aaron Rutledge, a new student to Roosevelt High, quickly gains a label from the teachers and staff as a new troublemaker. Though only a sophomore, he has been to a variety of schools in numerous states. Like other Rebels (male and female), Aaron is constantly defensive and is prepared to show that he doesn't care about what anyone thinks of him. He is determined to stay at this school only because he secretly yearns for some stability. In this chapter, Aaron debates the fairness of a tardy with his English teacher, Ms. Smith.

It is the fourth week of school, and Aaron has already gotten in trouble nine times—yes, he is keeping track; he always keeps track. At his last school he had been in trouble eighty-nine times before they expelled him. Aaron admits that eighty of those had been minor infractions and that everything—behavior, punishments, everything—always happened at a faster rate as time went by. To him, being in trouble is just a part of life. A person has to fight and *win*, or else he will be the first chosen when the next fight occurs.

Being in trouble doesn't have to mean fighting, but often it turns into that. Trouble always starts with a little *t* in Aaron's mind, but it quickly grows into capital, red, flashing letters. Unfortunately, these angry red letters come faster and faster as he grows older. Maybe it has to do with losing patience, or maybe it has quickened because of all of the teachers who haven't given him a chance and have never believed in him to begin with; but, whatever the cause, his parents have already given up on him, so there is little to lose—except for the slim hope that this new school will be different.

As he hurries from gym to English class, he thinks about his new school. The chances provided are fewer, and the rules are more stringently enforced; this is a new concept to Aaron. Specifically, this school enforces the three-strikes-and-you're-out policy. Other schools had that policy too, but with a little groveling, Aaron was masterful at earning another chance.

Aaron has already been to Dean Edwards's office four times since the beginning of school. The dean *clearly* said the next time he sees Aaron that he will be out for good, and Aaron believes him. He doesn't want to be put out of school again, mostly because there are no good options. Aaron looks old for his age, but he isn't old enough to join the army and doesn't think he can sustain lying about attending school when he isn't. His mom and stepfather aren't likely to move again since *The Step* finally got a job at a packing plant this past week. Furthermore, Aaron's mom works two jobs and is looking for a third, so there is no way that they will pack up and move again so soon—especially not for his anger issues.

> How can schools/teachers better help new students assimilate to a new environment?

Previously being *dismissed* from school was humiliating to Aaron; it implied that he wasn't smart enough or good enough for school. Early in his schooling, Aaron felt smart enough and capable enough. However, he just never felt like he fit into the system. So Aaron doesn't let himself think about how good he is anymore because, when he does, it triggers an anger episode that results in more trouble than he was originally in. Experience has shown Aaron that the deeper he gets into a situation the harder it is to get back out.

Aaron has learned the hard way; when he was in eighth grade, he flicked a pencil at someone's head. The teacher called him an idiot for doing something that could "poke someone's eye out," so he flipped her off and said, "I'll show you who's stupid!" Aaron grins at the thought now. He realizes that he has become more articulate since then, and he has *much* better aim.

The thing that most teachers just don't understand is that Aaron really doesn't like to fight. He prefers to sit in the back of the room and let everyone ignore him. But he learned after the first school change that blending in and avoiding attention was only a dream to him. At subsequent schools, teachers always asked the same questions: Where are you from? What do you like to do? Did you like your last school? What is your favorite part of school?

To impress students, Aaron always shares that he previously attended a school in the Bronx, that he likes to shoot in the park after school, and that his last school was cool because the teachers let them play poker during class. Even if this is a slight exaggeration of his last school, he likes to pretend that he has only ever gone to two schools — this one and his first school in the Bronx. Everyone knows that anywhere in the Bronx is a tough place to be.

Aaron quickly moves from one end of the building to the other, dodging squeaky girls, nerds, lounging hordes of athletes, and *normal* kids. In the process, he thinks about the teachers at Roosevelt High. The way he figures it, there are three types of teachers: those who have something to prove (they're smart, they're right, they're strong), those who are creative and open (usually wilt under pressure), and those who are overly interested in everything (in their subject, in thinking they can save the world, in knowing your personal life).

No matter what type of teacher he has, every single one of them has given up on Aaron. He tells himself that he doesn't care about anyone, but honestly he wonders what it would be like to respect someone and actually have that person respect him back. Aaron thinks it is probably impossible to find someone like that, but if there were such a person, maybe Miss Smith would be the one. He is going to her class next, and if he could pick up his pace just a little more, he might make it before the bell and get a handshake at the door similar to the one that surprised him the first day of school.

He has hurried for that handshake every day since then. It still surprises him that he will hurry for anyone, especially a woman teacher. As he does with everything that bothers him, he quickly pushes the thought from his mind. He turns the corner—only four more doorways and around one more nerd to get there! He knows that he can make it and even switches his books from his right to left hand so that he will be ready for the handshake.

How can teachers show that they haven't given up on a student? Is there ever a time when an educator should/must give up on a student?

Miss Smith stands in the doorway while glancing periodically into the classroom to make sure that everyone is settling down. She reminds them of their bell work *before* the bell actually rings so that class time won't be wasted. She smiles as she thinks about *her kids*. No matter how many weeks it has been, they still need that gentle reminder to stop talking and focus on the upcoming task. They probably will always need that little push, but that's why she loves working with the *regular* kids.

They can be unbelievably stubborn and often are unmotivated unless something directly pertains to their lives. Yet the things they talk about are often unexpected and enlightening even if not always appropriate. She glances once more out into the hallway and notices Aaron practically running down the hallway. She quickly shifts her attention to the clock on the far wall, only to be distracted by a student standing on the desk near the clock.

While Miss Smith contemplates the student standing on the desk, Aaron has made it past the four remaining doors and is just about to dodge the last obstacle before entering class. In the process, he barely clips a nerdy kid, who quickly sprawls on the floor with his books smashed underneath him. Aaron groans at the delay but spins around and pulls the kid to his feet. As Aaron turns back toward Miss Smith's class, the tardy bell rings. He tries to lunge through the door, but Miss Smith holds out her hand to stop him.

"You're tardy, Mr. Rutledge."

Aaron loses his breath from the shock. He takes three short, loud breaths and steps closer; she steps back. "But Miss Smith, I was right here!"

"You know my rules—in your seat when the bell rings," she says in a firm voice, looking past his shoulder.

As teachers, what battles are worth fighting? Is this a battle that should have been fought?

"I would have been but—"

"There are not excuses in my classroom, Mr. Rutledge."

"But I was helping that kid up!" Aaron says with growing aggravation. They both look down the hallway. The student is already scurrying around the next corner with his hallway pass gripped tightly in his right hand and trying to juggle four books and two binders in the other. He overcompensates and nearly falls over again as he rounds the corner at the end of the hallway.

"Hey! You! Get back here!" Aaron yells. His voice echoes down the now empty hallway.

Miss Smith says in a quieter voice, "Mr. Rutledge, I will not have you acting so inappropriately in the hallway."

"I'm not acting *inappropriately*; I just wanted his attention."

"That is not an appropriate way to get it."

"Yes, it is."

"I will not argue with you about this."

Aaron glances back to see the kid disappear around the corner and knows there is no chance to get him back, no chance to prove that he did something good—something that ordinarily would have caused Miss Smith to smile and offer him a pat on the back. Miss Smith sticks her head through the doorway and firmly reminds her students that they are supposed to be working on their bell work, a one-page journal entry on reaching for the stars. When she turns toward the students, Aaron tries to brush past her. She extends her slender arm and blocks the doorway. She glances once more at the students and then shuts the door as much as she can to prevent any more of a spectacle from erupting.

"You don't get to come in, Aaron. You must accept the consequences of your actions."

"But I was here! You saw me!"

"You weren't where you were supposed to be. You must go to Dean Edwards's office. I know this is your fourth tardy because after your third I made the required call home to your father at the beginning of the week."

"He's not my father; he's my stepdad. There's a difference!"

"Okay, okay, I made a call home to your *stepdad* on Monday."

"I don't care what you talked to him about! I'm not going to the office," he says in an angry tone with a stiffening body.

"You will, or I will call and have someone come get you. Don't make this harder on either of us; don't push this to the next level."

"You mean harder on you. You don't care about me. I can't go to the office—I'll be put out this time! The dean said the next trip to the office will mean that I'm out for good. I can't be put out of school again. You can't do this to me!"

"I'm not doing it to you; you did it to yourself. You should have thought about all of this before you decided to be late again to my class. At some point, you have to start taking responsibility for your actions; the real world doesn't put up with tardiness. Please go of your own accord."

By this point, Aaron's voice has raised an octave to match his increased panic. Shifting from one foot to the other, he thrusts his arms rigidly to his side. This defensive posture would look aggressive to many, but Miss Smith knows otherwise. Coach Wright enters the hallway from the room next door. He has prep this period.

"You starting trouble again, Rutledge?"

Aaron glares at him. He remains silent, but he turns his eyes back to Miss Smith. She refuses to look at him. With brightness in his eyes, Aaron turns himself to face Coach Wright squarely.

"I never start trouble, Coach," Aaron mutters.

"If you don't start it, it sure quickly finds you. Just yesterday I called your dad about your practice ethic. He said you were a lazy third-stringer at your last school."

"He didn't let me stay at the last school long enough to be able to play. Even when I could stay at a school long enough to play, he would never come and see a game." Aaron glances back to Miss Smith, who would not return eye contact.

> How can teachers be more proactive in working with angry students? How can teachers defuse anger once it has surfaced?

"I'm not saying anything else to you, and I don't care about her," Aaron says, referring to Miss Smith. Aaron lifts his chin a little higher and tightens his jaw, which is now beginning to tremble.

"You'll have something to say sooner or later," Coach Wright says with confidence.

Aaron doesn't back down. He stands looking neither at Miss Smith nor Coach Wright. As Coach Wright begins to reach out, Aaron flings his arm back to avoid his grasp. The coach grabs his arm on the second attempt. Aaron immediately slumps. His shoulders droop, his back hunches defensively, and his eyes hit the floor. Coach Wright says, "I'll take care of him for you, Miss Smith. We don't want third-stringers here—they bring down the team!" Aaron trails behind Coach Wright as they head toward the office.

> Is it ever appropriate to put a hand on a student—whether for authoritarian reasons or for encouragement?

How had the situation gotten out of hand? Miss Smith wonders. She thinks things are under control and then something like this happens. She doesn't want to get Aaron into trouble, but at the same time he has to learn. A person can't be late to work and not be punished for it. Miss Smith's guilt escalates.

She had argued with him, she had only seen black and white about an issue, and she had let another teacher—a male coach—take over her confrontation. These were all things she had promised herself she wouldn't let happen in her first year of teaching. Tears fill her eyes. *Count*, she thinks—*one . . . two . . . three . . . four . . . five . . . six . . . seven . . . eight . . . nine . . . ten. . . .* At the end, she sends one resentful glare into Coach Wright's now empty room and then reenters her classroom.

What are some strategies that can help new teachers deal with daily stress?

"Time's up for bell work. Turn to chapter ten of your book please."

INTERACTING WITH THE REBEL

The Rebel archetype provides an excellent forum to address the anger that resides within many of today's students. Anger can be a result of internal issues (classroom or school issues), external issues (family or personal issues), or a combination (friends, school, work, and/or family issues). Regardless of the origin of the anger, teachers who are effective in working with the Rebel find ways to sufficiently defuse anger, thus allowing the student to grow and succeed. Attempt to contextualize each of the strategies that follow into your own teaching environment. In so doing, you will find which strategies are likely to be most effective for you.

Earn Student Respect

A painful lesson for new teachers who grew up in a middle or upper socioeconomic background is the realization that respect is often earned—not given without question. For students that are streetwise, trust and respect is not given up front. Specifically, while some students will offer trust and respect on the first day, others will reserve judgment until six weeks or so into the first term. Students from high-poverty settings are more likely to reserve judgment. Realizing this cultural or socioeconomic difference can save teachers undue frustration. Furthermore, time previously spent on battles about getting students to adopt your cultural norm no longer seem necessary.

To begin building respect and trust, several things are imperative. Specifically, keep your word (unless personal safety for you or the student is an issue), be consistent in your treatment of students, and make every attempt to keep behavioral issues private (between you and the student). Remember that you do not like being chastised in front of a class and neither do your students. Find a moment before, during, or at the end of class to have any necessary personal discussions with students. A phone call home to the student is another great alternative. Make it clear why you choose to visit individually with them instead of addressing their behavior in front of their peers. When students see that you are on their team, respect is quickly earned—particularly when you honor your word.

Overcome Negative Attitudes

On days when multiple students enter class with negative attitudes or clear anger issues, three distinct options are present for the teacher: ignore it, refocus it, or confront it. When anger is ignored or denied, students typically shut down and totally disengage, or they become volatile and highly disruptive. When negative attitudes become endemic in the class as a whole, though not severe, try refocusing attention by having the entire class stand, grab their belongings, exit from the class, and then reenter with a more positive, constructive attitude.

Used sparingly, having students reenter the class can provide a quick refocusing. Be quick, concise, and effective as you redirect student energies. Without strong classroom management skills, you may compound the problem by adding disruption to the negative attitude. Such refocusing or visualization techniques help to handle minor or infrequent cases of anger. This brief activity lets students know that you acknowledge the difficulty of the day while still keeping high expectations relating to their success.

Incorporate Anger Management in the Curriculum

Incorporating stress/anger management techniques within the school setting or your class curriculum provides a way to proactively encourage positive self-esteem, lower stress levels, or lengthen the *fuse* before anger erupts. If advisory time is not available to work on such techniques, then find ways to integrate anger management techniques into your curriculum—particularly as part of having students learn to work cooperatively.

Just saying that students cannot work in groups is not sufficient. Maybe a better response is that they cannot work effectively *yet*. Helping students become successful in working cooperatively in groups is an essential component for improving learning and succeeding in the workforce. After all, poor interpersonal skills is the number one reason that people are fired from their jobs (Kagan 1997).

But what about today? What can you do with the Rebel? Having the Rebel sit at the front of the class provides more control for you as the teacher but often makes the Rebel feel closed-in and helpless. A possible effective compromise includes seating the Rebel near the door. With an established behavior contract, the student could be allowed to step outside the class for a few moments to regain composure instead of reacting inappropriately.

Practicing active listening techniques (also called reflective listening) can help encourage an environment of trust because the student feels heard and understood. After the student feels understood, then an action plan can be developed with clear consequences outlined. Part of anger management training includes helping students realize that some issues need to be set aside until an appropriate time can be found to discuss them. Explicitly letting students know when you will be able to hear their concerns may allow them temporarily and more appropriately to refocus on the task at hand until the issue can be properly addressed.

Another part of anger management training includes making sure that each student realizes his or her role in the success of the class. Students can help calm a situation, but they need to learn how and when to get involved and when to move away. Often students are able to defuse angry peers before things progress to inappropriate verbal or physical altercations. There may be times when anger issues are more significant (e.g., physical or emotional abuse). In such cases, a professional network (e.g., counselors, social workers, CPS) needs to be developed to assist, to guide, and to provide the necessary support to work through the issue.

Robert Marzano (2003) contrasts three different forms of anger shown by the Rebel: hostility, oppositional, or covert. Hostility is anger that includes rage, threats, or verbal/physical abuse. Oppositional anger assumes the opposing viewpoint and then forces others to adhere to their position. Covert anger slyly sets others up for failure, changes position at the last minute, or agrees and then does the opposite.

Knowing the different forms that the Rebel's anger may assume in class is important before skills can be developed within students that allow them to succeed. Remember, even though we are not hired to be counselors, we owe it to our students to help them successfully navigate the day-to-day interactions among teachers and students. Until a win-win situation is achieved between both students and teachers, work remains to be done. So how do we facilitate successful classroom interactions among students, particularly when anger is a significant issue?

Seek Collaborative Approach to Conflict Resolution

When working with angry and explosive students, three distinct options exist: (1) we can impose our strength and power by insisting that our expectations be met, (2) we can collaboratively engage in solutions with our students, or (3) we can reduce and/or remove expectations that we have for our students (Greene and Ablon 2006). The first option likely will only further embed the anger issue. When we assert our power over students, we may temporarily control the situation but respect is lessened and further outbreaks of anger are likely forthcoming.

Collaborative approaches to anger management may be time consuming, but if the behavior improves and the student engages in positive ways in the classroom, then it is worth the effort. Collaborative approaches ideally involve the student, parent(s), and current teachers.

However, the collaborative approach to conflict resolution can work nicely with just student and teacher if a positive rapport has been previously established. This emphasizes the importance of building strong relationships with our students before behavioral things interfere.

The final option to conflict resolution is to lower standards or expectations. This should be avoided even if it is only temporary. If students know that expectations will be lowered if they are disrespectful, show anger, or inhibit learning, then they are sure to increase the occurrence of the negative behavior. Typically, when a student misbehaves enough, he or she is removed from the traditional class and placed in a setting with high discipline yet low expectations for learning.

The collaborative approach to working with Rebel students seeks to keep expectations high while working through the obstacles that are blocking success (e.g., external issues from home, lagging cognitive skills). So how can anger be averted in the first place?

Create a Safe, Engaging Environment

Teachers cannot control all negative or aggressive displays of emotion that the Rebel may show. However, the environment that you create is the first critical step to possibly averting undesirable actions. Think about where tempers tend to rise. Road rage is an example that anyone living in or near a major city can relate to, even if they possess the kindest of spirits. The opposite emotional experience, one of tranquility and pleasure, can be seen when driving on an open road in the country, along the ocean, or in the mountains.

The first example incites anger while the second example abates anger and has a calming effect, yet the task of driving from point A to point B is the same in both examples. This implies that providing pleasing surroundings and enough space to work is vital in a school setting for optimal performance. For students with anger issues, we can help by providing opportunities for them to release or vent their frustrations. These release mechanisms can occur through guided journaling activities; conversations with peer mediators, teachers, or counselors; or time-outs that allow the student to remove him- or herself from a setting before it gets beyond control.

Criminologists James Q. Wilson and George Kelling provide another example of how environmental conditions influence behavior with their broken windows theory (Gladwell 2000). The premise of Wilson and Kelling's theory was adopted by former mayor Rudy Giuliani and the residents of New York City. The city's crime rate went from one of the worst to one significantly below the per capita crime seen in other major cities.

The plummet in crime rate began when the premise of the theory was addressed—a broken window left unattended sends a message that no one cares or is in charge. The ensuing anarchy that can evolve is related, at least in part, to the idea that seemingly small issues such as graffiti, a broken window, and general disorder become the floodgates that open the way for major criminal activity.

As I work with different schools and districts, the importance of the school environment is clear. When graffiti in the bathrooms, on desktops, and on lockers is tolerated, even slightly, the implications are profound and send a clear message to students regarding school climate. Positive school climate is seen when teachers, leaders, and students realize the clear correlation between the environmental conditions and the expectations held for the students, teachers, and administrators.

The message is clear—our schools need to be clean, orderly, and welcoming in ways that suggest a caring, safe environment. If damage or graffiti is spotted, it should be photographed for evidence and then removed before the next class period. As I walked into my first general chemistry teaching assignment, I was greeted with three years of unwashed glassware, dirty equipment, and storage cabinets that certainly hadn't been attended to for decades. Needless to say, cleaning was one of my first priorities.

Why should students be expected to come to class prepared and organized when the classrooms and the school exude signs of going out of business? It is not enough for teachers to care; the environment provides the external action that models whether or not a teacher and/or school cares. So are your words mere rhetoric or do you demonstrate that you care by creating an environment that encourages positive behavior?

Finally, the professionalism that we convey through our daily attire is another way to promote a positive environment. Dressing like students or in an unprofessional manner sends a message to students that we do not value them or the profession enough to dress professionally. Dressing the part conveys a confident, caring professional. Yes, there are days to dress to promote school spirit. However, on the other days, jeans, tennis shoes, and a wrinkly golf shirt are never respected by students—such attire provides another reason why our profession often lacks the respect it deserves.

Encourage Successful Group Interaction

In most cases, the anger evidenced by the Rebel is not a personal attack on us or even our students. Instead, we and our students become the venue for such students to release pent up emotions from other deeper issues. Until we know our students well, it is difficult to understand where the anger originates. Moreover, knowing our students well is the best proactive measure for averting major issues later. Even with effort, the cause of the anger will not always be known.

We are hired to teach students in our content domains (e.g., chemistry, English, U.S. history), but any solely content-driven classroom that negates the emotional, intellectual, and physical needs of our students will fall well short of optimal. Just as the physical environment must be developed, the intellectual, learning environment must also be fostered.

Most students do not walk into a biology class on the first day of school ready to work in dyad or triad cooperative learning groups. Furthermore, if the social, interpersonal climate is not well developed, then several things are likely to happen: (1) some groups will perform well while many will flounder because of poor communication; (2) students who come to class with anger issues will likely shut down, explode, or sabotage the overall success of the group; and/or (3) teachers will opt to always use direct instruction (e.g., lecture, worksheets, independent work) because they are frustrated with the lack of success seen by group interactions/learning.

Time must be made, particularly early in the school year, to allow our students to get to know one another and for us to get to know them as well. We can begin to understand students by conducting general interest surveys, having students write some form of an autobiographical essay, reading journal responses that contain personal comments, talking with students before or after class and/or listening carefully to what is shared with the entire class. Whole class or small group sharing are the only examples that actually help other students begin to know and to feel comfortable with one another.

So, as a teacher, we must first determine the class goals. For instance, if peer editing, working with lab partners, and/or studying and presenting collaboratively are important goals for the class, then we have a responsibility to help develop these skills in our students. Even as trained professionals, we have difficulty walking into a room of unknown people and immediately performing our best work in a collaborative setting. The same is true for our students. For the Rebel, who may quickly become agitated, anger is a defense mechanism preventing them from having to take a risk.

So goals for effective, dynamic classrooms include having students work successfully together in groups to learn and apply skills and knowledge. Furthermore, successfully collaborating is not a skill that students or teachers inherently possess; so what is the next step? First, be reminded of the importance of needing to work well together with different types and abilities of students. The main reason why people lose jobs is because of the inability to work well with others, not because of a lack of skill. If a primary goal is to help develop lifelong success, then we have to immerse students in group learning and not run from it because of challenges seen.

Whether respect is given or must be earned by the students, the need to develop meaningful, caring, and supportive relationships is invaluable.

Aaron provides an example of a student that was beginning to believe he had a fresh start, but his behavior, which is influential, became the roadblock. We will undoubtedly experience some setbacks as we work with students who are easily angered, but when students truly know that we care, the obstacles become smaller and more manageable.

REFERENCES

Gladwell, M. (2000). *The tipping point: How little things can make a big difference.* New York: Little, Brown.

Greene, R. W., and Ablon, J. S. (2006). *Treating explosive kids: The collaborative problem-solving approach.* New York: The Guilford Press.

Kagan, S. (1997). *Cooperative learning.* San Juan Capistrano, CA: Kagan Cooperative Learning.

Marzano, R. J. (2003). *What works in schools: Translating research into action.* Alexandria, VA: ASCD.

CHAPTER 2

The Socialite

October 11

Tina Hodges is described by her teachers as a great person but an overly distracted student. She prefers to leave academics to the "dorks." Socialites like Tina are highly influential and have the potential to lead in both positive and negative ways. Highly motivated by peer response, Socialites easily lose focus, and they quickly change allegiances depending on who is present at any given moment. In this chapter, Tina focuses on selecting her date for the homecoming dance while reflecting on classroom interactions from the prior week.

With butterflies in his stomach, Coach Wright wraps his headphones around his neck, grabs the playbook for his patented Steamroller Defense, and heads onto the field for the biggest game of the season—homecoming. The team is fired up to impress the parents, alumni, staff, and students who have shown their support all week by putting up signs on lockers, holding a parade, and even holding a pep session during seventh period. "Let's go, Cougars!" Coach Wright screams as he jogs onto the field.

Outside the stadium, Tina Hodges waits in the ticket line with Sam Fisher. After being dumped earlier in the week by her boyfriend, Tina needs to find a date quickly and Sam is a top candidate. Tina waits to see if Sam will pay for her—a telltale sign of his affection—and he does. She smiles, acknowledges the kind gesture, and begins secretly to hope he will ask her to tomorrow's homecoming dance.

Tina's preparation for the dance began months ago. She ordered a dress in July, found matching shoes in August, and set a hair appointment back in early September. The setback of being dumped by her boyfriend has really thrown a wrench into her plan. To remedy the situation, she is pursuing three possible dates for the dance. Since football games have four quarters, she is planning to give one quarter of attention to each prospective date, and then make her decision during the fourth.

As Tina reaches the ticket window, she sees Ms. Smith smiling back at her. "Hi, Tina!" exclaims Ms. Smith. "Have you finally picked a date for the homecoming dance?"

"Not yet, but we'll know soon enough," says Tina. "Hey! Wait a second! Why are you taking the tickets and not Mr. Nguyen? Doesn't he always do this?"

"His wife had a professional banquet that he had to attend."

"That's just like Mr. Nguyen. Someone needs to teach him to take it easy on the weekends. He should be here having fun at the game."

Tina thinks back to Mr. Nguyen's biology class and all the embarrassment that his "businesslike" persona caused her earlier in the week. The students had been outside collecting leaves for a photosynthesis lab when Mr. Nguyen had spotted Tina and Sam Fisher (the boy who took her to the game) exchanging cell phone numbers.

> When should teachers be concerned with "small things" like this, and when should they just let them go?

"I'll ignore it this time, but if I see it out again, I'll have to take it away," Mr. Nguyen said. "You're not supposed to have cell phones in the building."

Sam retorted, "But we're not *in* the building," and by this time, other students were starting to gather around, anticipating Mr. Nguyen's next move.

"Okay," said Mr. Nguyen. "If you want to give me a hard time about it, I'll just take it away now. You can have it back at the end of the day. I'd advise you to get back to work on your leaf project that is due Thursday and worth 10 percent of your overall grade."

Sam handed his phone to Mr. Nguyen and began to walk away, but Tina didn't let the argument end there.

> The student *wants* attention. In what ways can teachers enforce discipline without creating a scene for others?

"Mr. Nguyen, that's not cool. Doesn't he get a second chance?"

"He'll get a second chance tomorrow."

"Come on, Mr. Nguyen. I promise we'll start working on the leaves now. Maybe you could even switch the groups so that Sam and I can work on this together."

"No," said Mr. Nguyen. "The groups are set. Maybe we can do that on the next lab. Now get to work. We only have a fifty-minute period. Try not to waste any more of our time. I had to get permission to go outside again today."

Tina stormed off, and to get even, she decided not to work on the project at all. She randomly grabbed some leaves from random trees to make it look as though she were working, complaining the whole time to Adrienne, a possible sympathetic ear. "I think that was totally unfair. Mr. Nguyen wouldn't even listen to what I had to say. Plus, my cell phone number was on that phone. He'd better give it back or Sam won't be able to call me. Why do you keep doing this stupid assignment anyways?" asked Tina.

Adrienne went about her business picking leaves, trying to ignore Tina's rant. "Come on, Adrienne. Don't you care about Sam? I mean, you're not going to stand up for him?"

Realizing that ignoring the conversation was futile, Adrienne finally replied, "Look, Tina. Just do the assignment. I think Mr. Nguyen is pretty upset, and you don't want to risk a bad grade because of a cell phone."

"That's just like you to say that, Adrienne," said Tina. "I know Mr. Nguyen, though. He'll cave in and let me slide by anyways. I'll talk him into it."

Meanwhile, Mr. Nguyen went about business as usual, helping other students in the class with their projects. At the end of the period, he called the class inside, and noticed that Tina wasn't her usual self; rather, she was quiet and avoidant. Mr. Nguyen decided not to fight this battle. As soon as the bell rang, he knew that Tina would be someone else's problem until Thursday.

At the beginning of class on Thursday, Mr. Nguyen collected the assignments. Tina rustled through her papers as the other students passed their assignments up. This was a strategy she had been using since second grade. In fact, Tina even had a name for it: the *rustle and hustle*. Tina was quiet and pretended to pay attention. In actuality, she was writing notes to her friends. When Mr. Nguyen asked her a question, she replied, "I don't know," and Mr. Nguyen immediately called on someone else.

> How can a teacher ask questions to the class that ensure everyone is paying attention? What strategies encourage full class participation?

On Friday, when Mr. Nguyen handed back the graded assignments, he asked Tina why she hadn't turned hers in. Tina replied, "It must have gotten mixed up with some other students' projects. I swear I turned it in."

Mr. Nguyen hesitated. He wanted to trust Tina, but then he remembered what she had done in class earlier in the week.

> Should students have to earn a teacher's trust or should it be given?

"Tina, I'm going to have to give you a zero. I'm sure I didn't lose any of the assignments, and I distinctly remember you not working well when we were outside on Wednesday."

Tina began to panic. Maybe her "hustle" was getting a bit rusty. She would have to act fast. "That's not fair! I was trying to do it. I just work slower than the rest of the class, so I took it home and finished it. I swear I turned it in."

Mr. Nguyen didn't want to argue, so he gave in a bit. "Tina, I'll give you the weekend to do the assignment, but it's due first thing on Monday."

Adrienne interrupted, "But, Mr. Nguyen, it isn't fair to the rest of us. She wasn't working on Wednesday, and she'll still get the same grade."

Mr. Nguyen was beginning to lose his cool. He had material to cover and couldn't spend the entire class period arguing. There were thirty students in the class—twenty-eight of which were now losing their patience. They began talking quietly around the room. Mr. Nguyen knew he had to defuse the situation quickly, so he just said, "I'm not sure what grade she's going to get. We'll have to see. Maybe she'll lose 10 percent."

> What concerns should be addressed to the entire class and which should be handled individually?

"Thanks for the second chance, Mr. Nguyen," said Tina.

The *rustle and hustle* had worked for now, but as Mr. Nguyen began the lesson, Tina realized that she now had some bigger problems. With the game and the dance, how could she finish the assignment over the weekend? Tina guessed she would just take the zero or try to talk her way into another extended deadline. After all, it's not as though photosynthesis has any *real* applications in the world. Getting a date for homecoming was a priority, not looking at leaves under a microscope.

Mr. Nguyen, labeling a photosynthesis diagram on the board, wouldn't give the situation with Tina another thought until Monday. Why should he? Students trying to *work the system* are daily occurrences. Sure, it is frustrating, but in the end, the important thing is that the students learn and do the assignments, not that they necessarily turn all assignments in on time. So Tina would turn the assignment in a few days later—no big deal. Out of 135 students, some wouldn't turn in the assignment at all. Late was better than nothing.

At the football game, Tina can't believe it as she catches herself thinking about school. "Oh, my gosh. I am the biggest loser," Tina snickers to herself as the first quarter comes to an end. Sam has done quite a nice job in carrying a conversation, but Tina knows the other guys still deserve a chance. She spots Erik Drayer by the concession stand, so she tells Sam that she's going to get some popcorn and heads over toward Erik.

In line, Erik sees Tina approaching and signals her over. "How ya doing, Tina?" asks Erik.

"Fine, just looking for someone to watch the game with."

"Why don't you come watch it with me?" he says, and like that, Tina begins the second quarter of play. *Sam seems to be having fun with his friends, so he'll never even notice I'm gone,* she reasons.

Tina and Erik sit down in the stands. The conversation goes smoothly, but occasionally Erik runs out of steam and there is a long, awkward pause. These pauses begin to kill his chances as a viable homecoming date. Tina knows she won't be able to stand there and stare at him all night. She needs a date she can talk to.

During one of Erik's pauses, Tina hears a whistle come from the field and sees Coach Wright dash toward the referee like a bolt of lightning. Tina can't believe that Coach Wright is so passionate about anything. After sitting through his lectures for the past six weeks, she has begun to think of him as a cardboard cutout—someone that she doesn't particularly like, yet someone she doesn't particularly hate. Tina is amazed to see this cardboard cutout in action.

> How can teachers best bring their outside interests into the classroom?

Tina likes that Coach Wright doesn't seem to care when she text messages her friends during class or writes and passes notes. He seems to understand that notes and cell phones don't bother anyone. Why make such a big fuss over nothing? *He is so much cooler than Mr. Nguyen,* thinks Tina. *He and I understand each other. We're both fighting the same system.*

It is Coach Wright's philosophy that if it doesn't interrupt his teaching, it doesn't bother him. It's a catch-22 when students pass notes—either you stop the action and disrupt the entire class, or you allow the two students to continue quietly. Furthermore, he reasons that students are expected to be effective multitaskers in today's society. When Mr. Wright takes his classes to the computer lab, he sets up a class chat room to help students with the assignment. Sure, the students get distracted easily by the chat room, but occasionally students that don't talk will actually get involved in class.

> Is it ever professional to disagree with school rules/policies? If technology is "the real world" in action, then why is it often disallowed?

The referee blows his whistle to signal the end of the second quarter and Coach Wright looks up in the stands. He sees the student section, standing as usual, and thinks briefly about the job he will return to on Monday. Luckily, the students will be taking a quiz. This will provide a few spare minutes to go over stats from the game. Coach Wright has used the same quiz for several years. Monday he will head down to the copy room during prep, pick up the sports page, check the headlines, get a snack from the vending machine, make the necessary copies, and then head back to the classroom for second hour.

Coach Wright will be covering chapter 4 this week. This keeps them on schedule to meet all of the state standards. He looks forward to Wednesday—the day he always reserves for the computer lab—because he knows the students love using technology. He always spends a bit more time planning his lessons for Wednesday, and finds that the students usually respond well. If only every day were computer lab day—these are the easiest days to plan for since there are so many options.

In the regular classroom, it seems to Coach Wright that lecture and group work are the only options. Since it is too hard to get students engaged, he often gives up, favoring a lecture-style classroom. If the students are lucky, they can play Jeopardy on Thursday to study for Friday's test over ancient Rome and ancient Greece.

> How is technology often used as an "easy way out" for teachers? How can it be used effectively?

Tina realizes that Erik would be a poor date for the dance. But Sam Fisher is not a shoo-in yet. Chris Maccabee is the last suitor in the running. Tina realizes that this presents a problem because Chris is on the football field. Naturally, Tina can't go down there to talk to him, so she will have to find out from someone else whether or not Chris has a date for the dance. Tina scans the audience for someone to ask, and her eyes land right on Mrs. Maccabee, Chris's mom and Tina's math teacher. Tina makes her way over to Mrs. Maccabee and sits down.

"I'm sorry to interrupt. I thought I'd just stop over here to say hi," says Tina.

"Oh. Well, I'm glad to see you here. I hope Chris gets to play tonight," replies Mrs. Maccabee.

"Speaking of Chris, has he found a date for the dance yet?"

"Well, he's planning on going, but he's had quite a time finding a date," says Mrs. Maccabee. "Why do you ask?"

She knows why I'm asking, thinks Tina. *Maybe I should go with Chris*. After all, it sure would make her feel good. But, on the other hand, Mrs. Maccabee must not care *that* much about the dance.

Earlier this week, Tina distinctly reminded Mrs. Maccabee not to give any homework for the weekend, but, like the typical math teacher, she gave problems out of the book anyway. "It won't take long," Mrs. Maccabee said. "You'll have plenty of time to go to the game."

Tina had a comeback: "With the game, my hair appointment, dinner, and dance, how are we supposed to get things done? I mean, these are extracurricular activities that the school sponsors. Isn't that a good enough excuse? Besides, Mrs. Maccabee, weekends aren't for school. We spend enough time here as it is. Why devote more time to school while at home?"

"Oh, come on, Tina," replied Mrs. Maccabee, leaning on the overhead projector. "You have all day Sunday to do the assignment. You know, I usually take papers to grade wherever I go on the weekends. That way, whenever I take one of the kids to practice, I get a little bit of work done."

"Mrs. Maccabee. Are you implying I should take my math book to the dance with me?" laughed Tina.

Mrs. Maccabee laughed back, as did quite a few other students in the class, who had now taken Tina's side, chanting, "No homework! No homework!" Mrs. Maccabee looked around the room and couldn't help but think how mad her son Chris would be if he were given homework this weekend.

"Okay. I'll give in part of the way. We'll only do the even-numbered problems," said Mrs. Maccabee as the class roared and applauded. Mrs. Maccabee knew it was important to do the assignment, but on the other hand, she wasn't stupid. She recognized that the homecoming activities would take up quite a bit of time, so she gave in.

> What expectations should teachers have for students beyond the school day? Does homework represent the real world?

As the third quarter draws to a close, Tina realizes that it is decision time. She sees Sam sitting alone, and decides he is the best bet for the dance. She simply cannot risk whether or not Chris will want to go with her. Moreover, it might be strange to date her math teacher's son. More importantly, she knows her friends would never let her hear the end of it. Speaking of her friends, she will have to consult them first, but she feels that Sam will be the right choice.

INTERACTING WITH THE SOCIALITE

In Robert Fried's book *The Passionate Teacher* (2001), he shares an interesting interaction between a teacher and his students, whereby students estimate that about 24 percent of their fellow students fall into the category of *popular but not smart*. While not scientifically gathered, the example serves to remind teachers of the prevalence of the Socialite in our classes. Furthermore, this casting of students should be seen as a dynamic label and not one set in stone. The *popular but not smart* label may seem cruel, but students and teachers readily identify with the stereotype and often use it either implicitly ("he hangs out with *those* students") or explicitly ("she sure fits the stereotype of the dumb blond"). Teachers need to understand the needs of the Socialite before a successful solution can be crafted.

Before Socialites will desire to engage in school and learning in ways that earn a demarcation of being both smart and popular, teachers need to realize the power that peer influence has on student (and adult) behavior and ultimately academic performance. Additionally, teachers need to address their own preconceived notions regarding the abilities of Socialites. The first issue confronting teachers in working with Socialites is the need to understand that there is often a concern that status will be lost, or so they think, if they are academically successful and reach their potential. Additionally, many areas where Socialites possess expertise (e.g., friendship, loyalty, style) are not normally part of the curriculum. When careful thought is given to the needs of the Socialite, a positive and productive relationship can be developed.

Encourage Confident, Intelligent Learning Behaviors

Any experienced teacher has seen a Socialite assume the role of *Damsel in Distress* whereby the student will feign low ability even when she is more than capable. Tragically, by the time Socialites reach high school, they often become so proficient at the role that they convince everyone of their low aptitude, including themselves. Furthermore, as long as this behavior is enabled, students begin missing key concepts that perpetuate the cycle of underperforming. The discipline selected or gender highlighted can be switched and the scenario still holds true—Socialite underperforming in a guise to improve social status.

Similar to underachieving students such as the Player, the Downtrodden, and the Overwhelmed, which will be discussed later, Socialites miss attaining their full academic potential. The underperformance of the Socialite results not because of lack of ability but instead because focus is easily lost or never held in the first place. Unfocused attention toward academic success is the cost of excelling in the social realm for many Socialites. So how can Socialites successfully be engaged in the classroom?

Develop Socialites into Strong Allies/Leaders

First, it is important to realize that Socialites dramatically influence the climate of any classroom, for good or for bad; thus, developing positive rapport early is essential for a healthy class dynamic. In fact, if the 80/20 principle used by economists is applied to the classroom, it would suggest that 80 percent of the leadership in a given class will likely come from about 20 percent of the students (about six students in a class of thirty). Additional examples of how the 80/20 principle applies to many areas of life can be found in *The Tipping Point* (Gladwell 2000).

The teacher can greatly influence whether Socialites lead in positive or negative ways. In addition to your words, the demeanor and body language that you use while interacting with Socialites will facilitate or hinder positive rapport. Early in the term, mention with sincerity how much you value the energy and enthusiasm that the Socialite brings to the class. Moreover, indicate how instrumental they are in helping to create a *positive* classroom environment.

Before issues have time to develop to the contrary, provide Socialites with several specific examples of how they can positively influence the class: (1) encourage ideas of those who typically are quiet, (2) promote optimism in the class instead of negativity or whining, and (3) try to keep class discussions focused on the topic/concept being studied. Occasionally allowing for divergent, though related, discussions may help to enliven the emotional energy within the class by allowing students to discuss and explore issues that are relevant to them as well as the lesson being studied.

Demonstrate Sensitivity to Interpersonal Issues

To continue building this relationship, be sensitive to major social events like homecoming, a holiday musical production, or a regional basketball tournament. Such sensitivity may necessitate moving a project deadline or test back a day. Students respect teachers whose understanding of students transcends the daily classroom experiences and interactions. Better yet, plan ahead so that nothing actually needs to be moved. When planning ahead, explicitly mention to students why you opted not to schedule a major assignment on the day that conflicts with major events. One will never be able to avoid all scheduling conflicts, so provide students with the assignments and expectations for the coming week so they can plan accordingly and work ahead if necessary.

The need to develop strong rapport with Socialite students is twofold in purpose: (1) to meaningfully engage them in your class, and (2) to encourage using their inherent leadership qualities to maximize classroom interactions. When students are meaningfully engaged, their own learning is enhanced; when students become leaders, then the learning experience of their peers also becomes enhanced. It is no surprise that class dynamics vary from class to class. So why do some classes flounder while others thrive? The reasons are many but for classes that seem to *gel*, Socialites are likely leading in positive ways. Thus, it seems that Socialites are critical for healthy social interactions within classes, but how can their apathy toward learning be effectively addressed?

Unite Academics with Social Interactions

Socialites are anything but apathetic in the social realm; apathy develops when the academics become the sole focus and the interpersonal is neglected. Cooperative learning instructional strategies such as think-pair-share, developed by Frank Lyman (1981), provide a nice balance between personal reflection on knowledge and ideas, small group interaction to share and expand knowledge, and whole class discussions that collectively tie learning to bigger ideas. The think-pair-share learning strategy forces all students to reflect on their individual abilities and/or challenges regarding the content being studied, but then quickly immerses students into a dialogue with others as they are provided opportunities to express their knowledge to peers.

Socialites often process their ideas by stating them orally and then refining their thoughts once they have shared. To a teacher, when students process their thinking in external ways, their thoughts are often perceived as poorly developed. However, if teachers continue to encourage clarification through effective follow-up questions, then students are able to provide deeper representations of knowledge.

This tendency to cognitively process ideas in an external, social context is common for extroverted individuals. The Myers-Briggs (Myers, McCaulley, Quenk, and Hammer 1998) personality inventory is an example of an instrument used to assess whether individuals demonstrate extrovert or introvert tendencies. Think-pair-share provides an excellent balance of developing self-knowledge (intrapersonal) along with building knowledge and understanding through interaction with others (interpersonal). Grant Wiggins and Jay McTighe have identified self-knowledge as the highest level of understanding in their book *Understanding by Design* (1998).

Become Attuned to Teen Culture

Before we can encourage students to develop a strong self-knowledge, we really need to understand them well. This need is where we can learn from and with the Socialite. There is a fine balance between trying to be too hip and neglecting to understand the lens through which our students view the world. As teachers who care about our students both as individuals and as learners, we must understand more than how our students interact with our content domain of English, history, or science.

If you have taught for a while, you know teachers who try to be too vogue or hip with students. It is painful for both adults and students to witness. The reasons that teachers fall into this behavior can be severalfold. One they forget that students need strong mentors, not more friends just like them. Additionally, there is a perception, though misguided, that respect will follow if they can *rap it with their homeys* (students). Furthermore, for some it is a way for them to try to revisit their youth and resolve the challenges that they experienced.

CHAPTER 3

The Misfit
October 26

Katherine Sweetbriar, also known as Kate or "K8," doesn't seem to be actively involved in anything. She doesn't participate in class, let alone extracurricular activities. Like many Misfits, Kate dresses differently from other students. Kate's behavior in Mr. Nguyen's class makes her an outsider, seemingly by choice. After class, Mr. Nguyen finds a note that introduces him to a side of Kate that he had never previously considered.

Moments before class starts, Mr. Nguyen takes a deep breath and adjusts his slightly askew tie. He has worn a tie every day for the thirteen years he's been a teacher and for the previous five years that he worked as a research scientist. Before he left the research world, he was a member of a large research team actively studying stem cell behavior.

Mr. Nguyen notices four students flirting at the last set of lab tables. Students aren't what they used to be, he reminds himself. They don't have the work ethic, the intrinsic motivation, the academic integrity that they had even five years before. Mr. Nguyen loves teaching, but the reason he originally entered the teaching field is no longer what motivates him on a daily or even hourly basis.

> How often should teachers revise their educational statement (teaching philosophy)?

Mr. Nguyen has done a lot of self-reflecting in the past few years. He comes to school every day because it is something that he can do; if he can teach even a few students to be academically competent problem-solvers, then he has made his contribution to the future of mankind. Furthermore, if he can inspire intrinsic motivation in at least some of his students, then he considers his life worthwhile. That is his ultimate goal; at the end of his life, he wants to be able to say that he did something positive in the lives of his students as well as in his own life.

Although he knows that teachers respect him for his consistently high expectations, competence, organization, and dedication, he often wonders what the students really think of him. He desires solid, meaningful (intellectual) relationships with students, yet he has always been very careful to retain a strictly professional relationship between him and his students. When other teachers complain about students continuously arguing with them or rolling their eyes, Mr. Nguyen reflects and reminisces on his own students.

His students rarely misbehave; he thinks that maybe they are too indifferent to care enough to be mischievous. Mr. Nguyen scans the new list of lab groupings that he has just created. He understands the importance of changing classroom interactions from time to time, but he also desires to retain his sanity. Students have no idea how tiresome it is to keep things interactive and to provide variety while not letting social issues overtake learning. As he examines the list, his eyes pause on Kate Sweetbriar's name, K8 as she writes on her papers, no matter how often he discourages the informality. Mr. Nguyen has determined that there are two types of students—those who are science/technical minded, and those who are creative/artistic minded.

K8 undoubtedly fits the artistic mindset, which seems to make it even harder for him to connect with her. K8 is a student that Mr. Nguyen finds hard to relate to on *any* level. Some days she wears baggy black clothes with chains hanging from multiple places. Other days she wears tight clothes with bright colors and graphics that are sarcastic, that border on profane, or that are indecipherable. Her favorite shirt seems to be the one that says, *No Sense in Being Pessimistic—It Wouldn't Work Anyway*. A close runner-up seems to be the gray T-shirt with the rainbow writing exclaiming, *Earth First! We'll Strip-Mine the Other Planets Later*. Although Mr. Nguyen must admit that her shirts are often amusing, he contemplates whether she really understands the complexities of the *grown-up* thoughts that she displays as billboard signage each day.

Her fingernails are always black, and she wears striking makeup, the most dominant feature being the black rings that line her bright blue eyes. Mr. Nguyen thinks she looks like a *Procyon lotor*, the common North American raccoon, but he refrains from sharing such thoughts. K8 never asks for help; she never asks for anything. She doesn't come for tutoring after school or the Science Olympiad practices that Mr. Nguyen advises; to his limited knowledge, she is not involved in any activity—curricular or otherwise.

What is a teacher's responsibility for encouraging student involvement in extracurricular activities?

While contemplating K8, he suddenly realizes that she has not found a lab partner. The lab group is beginning to follow the lab procedures, but they are ignoring K8, who is leaning against the counter and staring out the window. Mr. Nguyen decides to make his way subtly over to K8. Beginning at the far side of the room, he weaves through the various lab groups, while remaining attuned to K8. Mr. Nguyen briefly pauses at several lab stations to refocus students that have strayed from the lab's objective. Although his room is normally quiet and efficiently run, it is often hard to get any of the students to stay on task when the Halloween Dance is just two days away.

What classroom management techniques keep students focused before or after major events?

Mr. Nguyen grimaces as he remembers that he was recently asked to chaperone the Halloween Dance. What would he do at a dance? He had always been *too busy* to go to a formal during his high school years. He didn't even want to imagine what it would be like. Mr. Nguyen wonders with whom K8 will attend the dance, or if she will go at all; he has never seen her say more than a handful of words to someone of the opposite sex and little more than that to a person of the same sex. Mr.

Nguyen wonders if she has any friends at all. Mr. Nguyen slowly advances from one lab counter to the next and appears to the group next to K8. This allows him to observe K8's group without his presence being noticed.

"K8, you want to join our group?" Romy asks while hardly glancing toward K8.

"No," replies K8 without moving her gaze from the scene outside the window. She quickly refocuses her thoughts to the business across the street where all the people are free to go about their business with no one watching their every move, no one judging their every action, no one writing every little thing on a notepad to be placed in a file later.

"Not that we really care, but who are you going to work with then? You know Mr. Nguyen won't let you get by without at least pretending to have a partner," Jacqulin says from the other side of Romy.

"Since you don't really care, I don't see why you really asked," K8 murmurs as she leans forward and writes "K8" in the moisture of the rain-dampened window. She begins to make swirls all around her trademark signature.

"Really, K8, just work with us. We both have As in here; you already know we'll do most of the work," Jacqulin shoots back.

"I don't feel like pretending today. Just leave me alone," K8 continues in her same flat tone. After overhearing their conversation, Mr. Nguyen decides to step in. He knows that K8 is not lazy, but she just seems not to care about anything.

Quickly and unobtrusively, Mr. Nguyen makes his presence known. "Hello, ladies. How is the lab coming?"

"Fine, Mr. Nguyen," Romy and Jacqulin chime nearly in unison.

"Ah, it looks good so far. K8, I don't see your name on here. Ladies, please make sure to put her name on the paper as well. I'll be back at the end of the period to make sure that everyone has contributed to the group." The quiet intensity of his voice causes K8 to turn partially around and glance at Mr. Nguyen. K8's glare fades to a smirk as she lowers her gaze to his tie; it is light blue with navy π signs. It would seem that he is trying to be *up with the times*.

What steps should an educator take if a student does not seem happy?

"Right, Mr. Nguyen. I'll get right on that," she murmurs. Springing to life at least momentarily, K8 confidently turns to her assigned partners; she slowly pushes off the counter by the window and then unexpectedly pulls the lab procedure out of Romy's hands. Before Romy can protest too much, K8 rapidly scans the last several questions of the lab assignment and proceeds to rattle off the answers with bold confidence. K8 then tosses the paper back to the girls and smirks as Jacqulin grabs a pencil and begins to painstakingly work out the problems on a separate piece of paper.

How can educators make sure that group work is equally shared? How do we know if each student "gets it"?

Mr. Nguyen's attention gets redirected to two girls who are upset because they apparently bought the same dress, or something equally inconsequential, as far as he can tell. The bell rings before he works his way back to Romy, Jacqulin, and K8.

"Ladies and gentlemen, don't forget to finish this report for tomorrow!" he bellows as students scramble to grab bags and rush out of the door.

"Push in those chairs, Melanie and Samantha!" he adds when they nearly forget while grabbing their hot pink purses and brightly covered books. Mr. Nguyen sighs over being caught by the bell before students have properly cleaned their lab stations.

As Mr. Nguyen quickly moves from the back of the room to the front (straightening misaligned desks along the way), he sees K8 grab her notebook and pencil (the only things she ever brings to class) and head out the door. As she leaves the room, Mr. Nguyen notices that K8 has dropped a piece of paper. He hopes to retrieve it and return it to her before she is completely swallowed up by the human chaos in the hallway. Mr. Nguyen takes a deep breath; even though all teachers are supposed to have hall duty, he loathes stepping out into the anarchy called passing period.

> What strategies are good to ensure that students work until the end of the period? How much time is sufficient to encourage strong lesson closure?

When Mr. Nguyen gets to the doorway, his quick search down the hall reveals an endless stream of bobbing female ponytails and numerous uncombed male heads of hair that each resemble a nest of a unique species of bird. Mr. Nguyen shakes his head at the apparent demise of the human population. How did it ever become appropriate for boys to wake up and come to school looking like they just rolled out of bed? Mr. Nguyen sees the easily distinguishable short, bright pink and purple spikes of K8's hair, but she is now too far away to call for her attention in a suitable way. Although against his better judgment, curiosity wins out and Mr. Nguyen opens the folded paper that K8 dropped.

> When should a student's privacy be respected, and when should it be disregarded?

The first half of K8's paper is a black-and-white sketch, a remarkable portrait of herself. The right side has been made into a detailed likeness, complete with spikes, eye rings, and solemn mouth. Oddly, the other half is shaded and smeared, almost cloudy in appearance. On this second half, the mouth is tilted downward, and there is a large glistening tear on the rounded portion of the cheek.

The sketch makes Mr. Nguyen's heart skip a beat. He is suddenly hit by the sadness of K8, rather than the listlessness that he normally notices. Mr. Nguyen then reads the poem that is artistically written below the drawing:

For the Dead

—Adrienne Rich

I dreamed I called you on the telephone
to say: BE KINDER TO YOURSELF
but you were sick and would not answer

The waste of my love goes on this way
trying to save you from yourself

I have always wondered about the left-over
energy, the way water goes rushing down a hill
long after the rains have stopped

or the fire you want to go to bed from
but cannot leave, burning-down but not burnt-down
the red coals more extreme, more curious
in their flashing and dying
than you wish they were
sitting long after midnight

What are the steps that a teacher should take when he or she thinks that a student may endanger herself or others?

As the warning bell rings, Mr. Nguyen is jolted back to the world of chaos. David Sanchez, his resident Overachiever, is standing in front of him with Señora Hernandez at his side.

"Mr. Nguyen, I've been trying to explain to Señora Hernandez that the resident population in Madrid does not have the same biological attributes as the population in Mexico City, but she doesn't believe me. Can you enlighten her *please*?" David says with complete confidence.

"David, both you and Señora Hernandez are correct. I will explain it to you at the end of the period, once you have completed your activity. Now please go prepare for class," Mr. Nguyen murmurs with a distracted look still on his face.

"Isn't it funny what students are adamant about? Have a good day, Tony. I'll see you at lunch," Señora Hernandez chuckles as she makes her way back down the hall to her classroom. Mr. Nguyen rereads the poem once more before he puts it in the left pocket of his dress shirt and then returns to class.

INTERACTING WITH THE MISFIT

The reasons are many and varied, but some students just do not seem to *fit* well—particularly in certain classroom settings. Sometimes the reason is as simple as possessing different interests from the norm. Sometimes students are pushed out of groups because they view the world differently from their peers. In such cases, a student may feel marginalized and like an outcast in a class that has lots of athletes if his passion resides in music, theater, a unique hobby, or academics.

The feeling of being different from others may result in feelings of lack of acceptance through subtle or overt comments from teachers and students. Healthy classrooms accept and encourage these diverse differences among students. Diversity issues need to extend beyond the typically explored topics of race, gender, socioeconomic background, or religion. Maybe the goal should be to focus more on appreciating the differences that people all possess instead of seeking to develop a norm where all *fit* into a particular mold. If there is a desire for a supportive environment, then there are implications for how teachers should conduct learning in the classroom.

The cause and the effect often is difficult to know—are students cast aside because they are different, or do they choose to be different so as to stand out? Knowing the answer to this quandary is particularly challenging during the teen years. In one sense, students seek acceptance from their peers. In another sense, they are pushing away from teachers, parents, and various groups of students as they assert their independence. Students that adopt the gothic persona provide an excellent example of those who represent diverse ideals. The popularity of the trend that began in the United Kingdom in the 1980s has followed an ebb and flow pattern in schools throughout the United States during the past two decades, but one thing is clear—the visual statement is hard to avoid: black and charcoal colors dominate clothing selection, fingernail polish, and even makeup decisions, such as lipstick.

Driving to work the other day, I witnessed three gothically clad teens strolling toward a local high school. Two of the students displayed colorfully spiked Mohawks; all were wearing leather coats; and all were generously adorned with piercings that included noses, lips, ears, eyebrows, and I am sure a tongue or two. Complementing these bold statements of individual expression, one student had the word *acceptance* and another had *reality* spray painted in crude lettering across the back of their expensive leather coats. The juxtaposition of these two words was interesting. *Acceptance* appeals to the desire to belong to a community of others who are different while *reality* seems to suggest an attitude of "see me for who I am or don't see me at all."

The Misfit persona is manifested in various ways, but students following a gothic ideal willingly display their uniqueness. Punks, jocks, skaters, goths, thespians, preppies, or geeks, regardless of the label affixed to them, all want to be respected and cared about in significant ways by both teachers and peers. Even if defensive walls have been erected, all desire to belong to a social unit. The hope is to create an environment where all are respected and all are respectful of the similarities and differences held by others.

Celebrate Diversity of Expression

Diversity is often seen through a very narrow window—typically racial diversity. The Misfit suggests that we broaden this perspective to include those with ideas or viewpoints that are different from the norm. In business and industry, various viewpoints are encouraged as teams are assembled and then challenged to think innovatively regarding a concept or product.

Any assignment or activity that encourages students to consider an issue from a new perspective, other than their own, helps broaden everyone's viewpoint. For example, in a history class have students explain how a major historical event like the John F. Kennedy assassination

could have been perceived from the viewpoint of a wealthy political figure, a minority who lived in a small Texas community, your mom or
grandmother, or a fifteen-year old student in suburban America. Alterna-
tively, in a communications class, speeches could be tailored for specific
audiences such as easily bored teens, community members who oppose
your viewpoint, or experts on the topic.

Facilitate Meaningful Discussions among Students

Marzano (2003) categorizes Misfits as socially inept. Attempts to
make friends are often thwarted because of their appearance or behavior. Furthermore, their history is one that has been filled with teasing,
ridicule, and then isolation.

Misfits are often bright, witty, and talented. Somehow these talents
become masked by poor social interactions that result in peers' intentional or unintentional rejection or by isolation caused when the Misfit
picks inappropriate battles to fight. In many ways, the Misfit shares
many characteristics with the Invisible that will be discussed later. A
key difference is that Misfits often stand out so boldly in their actions
or attire and are ignored because of the attention that they seek. Because they have assumed or been cast into the role of Misfit for many
years, by the time they reach high school, they often forget the cause
that they support or oppose.

Since Misfits often have difficulty with social interactions, teachers
need to encourage and model successful interpersonal interactions with
these students. Rebels and Misfits are similar in that they struggle with
social appropriateness. Where the Rebel attempts to hide his social and
academic deficits in angry outbursts, the Misfit has difficulty knowing
what is appropriate for the audience. For instance, Misfits who are extremely bright often display their social ineptitude when working in
groups or classes where the rest of the audience does not share their
gift. Misfits may be able to answer a question on a test, but they often
have difficulty explaining in writing or more commonly through oral
expression the process of how they solved the problem.

For years, I have argued against the elitist separation of students by abilities. Proponents of segregated learning argue that the slower learners hold back those who process information quicker and who *get it* the first time. The reality is that there is much more to learning than just quickly responding to an answer. Richard Feynman, the Nobel Prize winner in physics in 1965, stated that we really do not understand something until we can explain it to the average person. This critical ability to clearly communicate our ideas is lacking from many bright students—particularly those who are challenged by interpersonal interaction. Often these Misfits know how to solve a complicated math problem or respond quickly to factual ideas, but they are not well equipped to explain ideas and concepts to their *less able* peers.

Let's face it—learning is typically shallow even in our most advanced classes. Specifically, learning is relegated to factual knowledge instead of strong conceptual understanding. Two examples illustrate this point. Most any K–12 student will respond to the following question in a similar fashion: What evidence do you have that the Earth is spherical and not flat (base response on information available prior to the space age)? The initial giggles and snickers at the seeming absurdity of the question quickly give way to sobering expressions when students recognize their lack of solid evidence. "My fifth grade teacher told me so" does not count for strong evidence—in fact, your fifth grade teacher may not know why either.

We quickly see that what appeared trivial was built on a shallow foundation of knowledge. This one seemingly simple question provides a great opportunity to integrate history and science disciplines. Furthermore, critical thinking and reasoning skills become central to the discussion. Because many will want resolution to the above question before proceeding, I will provide three words to help guide your learning: Eratosthenes, Columbus, and the moon.

The second example comes from a study of Harvard graduates who were asked another *simple* question to check for conceptual understanding on the day of their graduation (Harvard-Smithsonian Center of Astrophysics 1997). In one hand is an acorn and in the other is a log from an oak tree that was cut down. The question is: Where did most of the material come from to produce the log?

Once again snickers usually give way to major misconceptions in the basic knowledge that we were taught throughout school. Still donning their caps and gowns, most graduates, including science majors, missed the question. Maybe encouraging more thoughtful discourse among our students regarding the concepts being studied is worthwhile in terms of both improving the quality of learning and improving the communication skills of our students. Without directly answering the question, water and/or the soil are the most often cited responses. However, they are incorrect.

Provide an Encouraging Environment for All

Rarely are Misfits truly loners. Instead, Misfits may be outcasts in one or several environments but then feel at home in others. A *jock* may lack like-minded peers in an upper-level mathematics course but then come alive during soccer practice; an introverted *nerd* may feel isolated and unequipped to excel in a communications class despite a powerful intellect; or a *thespian* may be teased or feel her creativity is shunned in a science course. Everyone has environments where he or she feels more at ease. For some, an overabundance of environments where they feel detached makes school a daunting place to succeed.

One way to create a welcoming, more inclusive environment is to adapt assignments in ways that encourage the diversity of students. For instance, the thespian might desire to become engaged if the assignment and assessments are broadened to include an expression of creativity. Instead of having students just report their findings from a science experiment to class, they could present a report to the city council (real or fictitious). The assignment still should have students focus on key conceptual ideas, but the parameters for communicating ideas can be widened. These examples can be extended to all disciplines. A speech given in a communications class could be written for an audience that is diverse in a significant way from the presenter's actual viewpoint. Students should employ technology, classmates, or community resources to help strengthen their understanding of the audience to whom they will be communicating.

Remember when working with Misfits that they have hopes, dreams, and aspirations just like other students, but they often do not know how to connect in meaningful ways, particularly when they bring a minority viewpoint to the class. Just like with the other archetypes, strategies that work with one group often will work well with others. However, some strategies may have a greater affect on some personalities than others.

REFERENCES

Harvard-Smithsonian Center of Astrophysics. (1997). *A private universe: Minds of our own* [DVD].

Marzano, R. J. (2003). *What works in our schools: Translating research into actions*. Alexandria, VA: ASCD.

CHAPTER 4

The Overachiever
November 1

David Sanchez is actively involved in numerous extracurricular activities and his name resounds in the halls as the "Who's Who" of Roosevelt High. Though only a sophomore, David has his high school and college future meticulously planned. Like other Overachievers, he constantly checks his grades, attempts to complete all work accurately, and tries to please and develop a relationship with every teacher in order to ensure an A in the class. In this chapter, David questions his second nine weeks English grade.

On this Friday, Mr. Nguyen prepares to pass out the mid-term progress report for the second nine weeks to his last period class. Some students anxiously wait; others try to avoid the inevitable and nonchalantly drag themselves to retrieve the report from Mr. Nguyen's hand at the front of the class. David Sanchez is one of the anxious. He nervously taps one foot against his desk as he awaits the paper that contains the key to his future. Mr. Nguyen finally calls, "Sanchez." David walks to the front and clutches the progress report.

Back at his desk, David begins to inspect the report as others chat around him. He skims the grades for all seven classes; satisfaction turns to disbelief as he sees a C boldly printed next to Ms. Smith's English class. It's not like David is *above* earning a C. He just knows that anything less than a B greatly limits his chances for attending medical school one day. He knows that the grades he earns now greatly affect his chances of attending a prestigious Ivy League school and continuing on to a well-known medical school. David does not realize his standard is not high enough—prestigious schools expect all As, not Bs— especially if the goal is an Ivy League school.

David's face clouds over as he realizes that his second progress report of the year is tarnished because of Ms. Smith. The bell rings and the students clamor to the door. Though it is a Friday, David grabs his bag from his locker and makes his way to Ms. Smith's room.

> How do educators help students understand that grades are earned, not given?

Ms. Smith is sitting at her cluttered desk after a long day of teaching. Piles of student papers, clipped together by class, are stacked high on her desk. Her grade book and lesson planning book sit openly displayed on her desk. The Promethean board displays student edits from an intentionally error-laden paragraph analyzed during the previous period. A long list of e-mails that need attention fills the computer screen. Framed pictures of her college sorority days have been shoved between the desk and the wall as her mess grows.

> Which organizational characteristics are critical for effective classroom management and student learning, and which are merely individual characteristics of the teacher?

Ms. Smith is exhausted. Today's sunny, warm weather replaced the two previous cool, rainy days. The better weather plus the approaching fall break seemed to add to the rowdiness of the students today. A drink with an old college friend last night meant that Ms. Smith was up until 1:00 a.m. grading papers so they could be handed back before the weekend. She normally didn't do anything on school nights, but her friend was only in town for the night, so she made the exception. The only positive aspect about waking up at 5:30 this morning was the fact that it was a casual Friday. Casual Fridays meant hair pulled back into a ponytail, comfortable jeans, and a familiar T-shirt from her pre-work days. Unfortunately, casual Fridays also meant that Ms. Smith was sometimes mistaken for a student.

> How do educators, particularly younger ones, maintain professionalism while still being perceived as friendly?

As Ms. Smith begins to transfer the Odyssey papers that she must grade into her brown leather bag, she hears a steady, firm tap on her door.

"Come in," Ms. Smith calls out in a tired voice as she looks to see who the visitor is.

"Ms. Smith, may I talk to you for a minute?" David politely asks.

"Absolutely." Ms. Smith does not like to turn students away—even if it is a Friday.

"Pull up a chair, David. What is it that you want to talk about?"

"Ms. Smith, I'd like to see a printout of my grade. You gave me a C in your class, and I don't think that's right. I received a B on my last paper and an A on the assignment before that; therefore, I don't think my grade is correct. I've given this class my best effort, kept track of most of my grades, and tried really hard, and it's not fair that you gave me a C!"

> How do teachers ensure that the grade earned by students conveys their knowledge and understanding relative to the course goals or standards?

Ms. Smith knows that David is accurate on the account of his work ethic. Coming from Guatemala to the United States was a big transition for David. He works diligently on his writing and speaking skills. He stays after school, asks questions constantly, and always attempts each assignment. In his journals, David writes about how he struggled to learn the culture along with the English language when he first arrived in the States in the seventh grade. Sometimes the wording in his papers is still not correct, but his ideas are dynamic and well-supported. David is in Ms. Smith's only section of Honors English.

"David, keep in mind this grade is just a progress check. The grade is not permanent, and you can work to improve it before the nine weeks end."

"I can't have any type of C, Ms. Smith," David counters. "My future is riding on my grades. As Mrs. Johnson says, every grade matters if I want a full scholarship to Duke University. I know I did better than this, Ms. Smith. Check your grade book."

David's voice changes pitches as he begins to panic. His face begins to redden. Ms. Smith has seen this face before. Anytime David doesn't understand a concept in class, his face reddens to a deep crimson shade.

What are some specific steps that teachers can take to calm a student who becomes overly emotional?

As David continues his pleadings, Mrs. Maccabee and Señora Hernandez walk into the room to wish Ms. Smith a great weekend.

"David, what are you still doing here on a Friday?" Señora Hernandez asks as she enters the room holding her work for the weekend.

Señora Hernandez's arms are full with videotapes that she is planning to review over the weekend. She is known throughout the school for her artistic projects and her chaotic, disheveled room. Her room looks as if the Tasmanian Devil whirls through it before first period every morning—papers and art supplies everywhere. Textbooks are not frequently used, according to Señora Hernandez, because they stifle creativity, so they are typically strewn about the room. Señora Hernandez makes up for this mess with the remarkable poster-size pictures from her annual trips to Spain that adorn her walls. The people she meets and sites she visits are forever ingrained in each graduate's mind. The pictures pique the students' interest; they form the basis for many assignments, and they provide an easy way for students to get her off topic.

The latest project assigned by Señora Hernandez was to videotape a commercial in Spanish for a fictitious product. David and his classmate John had chosen to promote a magical pill that makes girls fall in love with whoever ingests the pill. They hoped that this fictitious product would somehow improve their unfortunate reality of having no luck with girls. Even knowing two languages hadn't helped David. Whenever he complimented a girl in Spanish, she gave him a blank stare and walked away. Didn't girls find actors like Antonio Banderas *hot*? He just didn't understand the difference. After creating the commercial, David and John had decided that if there actually ever were such a pill, they'd be the first to buy it *and* buy stock in it as well.

David brings his mind back to Señora's question as to why he's still at school on a Friday afternoon.

"I have a C in Ms. Smith's class, and my dad will kill me if I bring this grade home to him," David responds in a voice that clearly conveys that Ms. Smith is in the wrong.

David is immensely worried. His parents came to the United States to begin a business venture. The business is successful and his family does not struggle for money; however, with five children in the family, a scholarship is his only option to attend a college other than the local community college twelve blocks from his house.

Mrs. Maccabee tries to console him. "David, no grade is permanent. You have a bit of time to raise your grade before the semester is finished."

David only half listens to Mrs. Maccabee's words before he responds, "Mrs. Maccabee, I know that this grade isn't permanent, but there's no way that I received a C in English. I worked too hard to earn anything less than a B. I even made sure my work schedule and the Hispanic Club did not interfere with the due dates for the paper in Ms. Smith's class."

> How can teachers help students become more self-reflective about their school work?

Though only a sophomore, David is president of the Hispanic Club. Arriving at Roosevelt High last year, he was astonished to learn that there were a variety of clubs but not a single club that brought together Hispanics. With Mrs. Johnson's sponsorship and the school's endorsement, David began the Hispanic Club second semester last year. The club met bimonthly but wasn't anything too serious. The Hispanic Club typically met at an authentic Mexican restaurant. Plus, they organized fund-raisers to sponsor families in a poverty-stricken Mexican city.

David wasn't completely sure of the club's purpose. He only knew that it helped others get involved, helped people outside of his school, and, most importantly, helped build his credentials for college applications.

Ms. Smith firmly states, "David, I appreciate your concern for your grade, but it's Friday. Go home. Come talk to me Monday after school. By then, I'll have a grade printout for you, and we can sit down and discuss how your assignments, papers, and test scores influenced your grade. Does that sound like an okay plan to you?"

> Should an educator ever change a grade when under pressure from a student, parent, or administrator? How flexible or firm should a grade be?

David responds in a flat, disappointed tone, "Yeah, I guess so. I'll stay after on Monday, and we can talk about it then."

"Then it's a plan. I'll see you on Monday. Enjoy your weekend, David," Ms. Smith replies in a forced cheerful voice.

"You, too, Ms. Smith." David quickly grabs his navy backpack and black, oversized swim bag as he leaves the room.

Ms. Smith breathes a sigh of relief, and her body visibly relaxes as she rolls her neck from side to side to relieve the week's worries.

"Well, that's done," Señora Hernandez quickly states as if to sweep the confrontation out of the way. She brushes a piece of hair behind her ear, which causes her to lose the precarious balance she holds on the videotapes. Three come crashing to the ground before she can save them. The thud of plastic hitting the floor jerks Ms. Smith out of her temporary utopia.

"That's probably only the beginning," Ms. Smith states. "My grades were low compared to the other English teachers' reports. I'm sure I'll have more students in here on Monday wondering why they received the grades they did, despite the fact that they were told to keep a grade tracking sheet."

"Don't worry, Kim," Señora Hernandez interrupts. "It's the weekend. Take some time to relax. Everything will be waiting for you when you come back on Monday."

Ms. Smith sighs. That is just it; she knows that it all will be there when she returns on Monday. Why did it seem that all of her school problems followed her home—no matter the day?

INTERACTING WITH THE OVERACHIEVER

Unlike apathy that often originates outside the classroom (e.g., the Rebel), the educational system must assume some responsibility for the apathy conveyed by the Overachiever. Even though we should strongly support meaningful assessments of our students that are developmental, formative, and process-focused, we are seeing signs of testing and assessment fatigue in our students. Presently, there exists a ravenous state of quantifying, labeling, and evaluating everything that moves without having a clear focus of what we are doing. This unfocused obsession of quantifying everything greatly encourages the Overachiever archetype, who diverts attention toward grades and away from learning.

The Overachiever is not curious about learning, creating, exploring, and developing new ideas. Instead, energy becomes channeled to a product-driven, hunt-and-seek game between the Overachiever and the teacher. The myopic focus of the Overachiever prevents him from seeing anything beyond the specifications outlined in the assignment or rubric. The perfectionistic tendency of the Overachiever is not close to being a noble effort to produce the best possible work because the mental energy is not on the work. Instead, the student gets lost in the web of documentation that seeks to guarantee that successful mastery will be awarded. The cost of perfectionism includes meeting the letter of the law of the assignment but neglecting learning or applying knowledge in meaningful ways.

The apathy expressed by the Overachiever is unique from the other archetypes highlighted because it transcends all the levels of academic performance. Though unique in its manifestation, this archetype may be the most prevalent form of apathy in high schools today. The Overachiever archetype often overlaps with other typifications of apathy such as the Player, the Downtrodden, or the Invisible, which will be discussed later.

Ultimately, the Overachiever is the student who completes worksheets, labs, and activities while the brain remains largely disengaged. Learning becomes a game of amassing the required facts without ever mentally processing the material. The Overachiever is illustrated in the following examples: (1) comparing answers with several groups during a science lab in an effort to provide the best answer; (2) asking questions of the math teacher until she relents and just gives the answer; or (3) teaming together like vultures with other Overachievers whereby willing sources are questioned until the needed answers have been extracted. Disagreements between teachers and Overachievers typically center on grades instead of ideas.

The Overachiever is constantly looking for a way to justify a higher grade—not because they even feel their answer is right, but rather because they see an opportunity to gain a few points because of a perceived weakness in the system: "Johnny also put *b* for #3 and he got it right, but I got it wrong"; "It was not fair that you took off a full letter grade—there were only three errors in a three-page paper"; "The test was unfair because there were things on it that we haven't seen before"—specifically missing the point of the question that asked the student to *apply* his knowledge to a new situation. Whether the claims are correct or not, finding legal loopholes supersedes efforts to improve the quality of work.

Perfectionism, for the Overachiever, centers primarily on extrinsic motivation issues that value only the final prize of high grades (often higher grades than earned). Teachers grapple with this apathy archetype for several reasons. On one hand, we want our students to succeed academically (often denoted by grades), but on the other hand, we become frustrated when students lack enthusiasm for learning and avoid being challenged at all costs.

So why argue with good grades? After all, they are doing the work, so why question something that is not broken? The lack of desire to learn is what is broken. This lack of desire leads to an apathy that usurps the student's positive energy that otherwise could be directed toward learning. The goal of educators is to promote what Ellen Langer refers to as mindfulness (Littky 2004). Effective, meaningful learning is about getting students to grow their minds with ideas and thoughts. It is not about satisfying the requirements so that the letter of the law is fulfilled. So how can the pattern of compliance be replaced with a more meaningful engagement of the learner?

Emphasize Excellence Instead of Perfectionism

On the surface, the difference between excellence and perfectionism many seem small, but a vast chasm separates these two ideologies. Perfectionism is a mental attitude geared toward reducing risk and embarrassment so much that the student's best work is rarely, if ever, produced. Overachievers forgo their best work in favor of safe, carefully calculated attempts to meet the assignment expectations while minimizing meaningful critique of their work that could promote deeper learning.

Excellence, not perfectionism, requires a willingness to take a risk. Excellence can assume many forms. Some examples of excellence include: (1) a student who goes beyond the expectations of the assignment because she is truly interested; (2) a student who seeks an alternative solution or viewpoint; (3) a student who takes time to deeply reflect on what he or she has done; or (4) a student who learns from the experience and improves future performance instead of becoming defensive and argumentative. Those pursing excellence all share a common bond of using goals, standards, and expectations as the starting point or foundational structure to help frame their work. Perfectionists build protective moats around the content standards and assignment expectations, thus not letting their learning transcend beyond these intended foundational parameters.

As teachers we can help students realize that perfection can never be attained (except maybe on content-only tasks such as vocabulary tests). By attempting to pursue perfection, large amounts of energy often get misspent on the minutiae of the assignment instead of on the critical aspects of learning that were the goal of the assignment in the first place. As a teacher, it is important to be clear and consistent about expectations regarding work. Once those expectations are known, then little time and energy needs to be devoted to issues such as how long should it be, should it be single spaced or double spaced, or how many sources are needed.

Oddly enough, the commonality between perfectionism and excellence resides in the assessment portion of the work. Both seek high merit, but the perfectionist is self-critical, avoids the new and unknown, and possesses a narrow vision of learning. Those pursuing excellence constantly seek input from others, thrive on new ideas, and use rubrics and standards to guide their work, not limit it. Once the *habits of mind* (Meier 1995; Sizer 1992) become an integral part of the classroom, students begin to do more than obligingly fill-in-the-blank on social studies worksheets, parrot back algorithms in math, or reproduce prescriptive labs in science.

These habits of mind require teachers and students to provide evidence, consider a differing viewpoint, develop suppositions, and integrate relevance in authentic ways. If we as teachers cannot incorporate these habits of mind into the majority of the curriculum, then we should question why that particular concept or idea is taught. Teaching solely because it *covers* an item on the standardized test misses the point of education and neglects the role of the teacher. Please do not misconstrue this to suggest that concepts found on standardized tests are unimportant or irrelevant; they become irrelevant when they are taught in isolation without a deeper context. Teaching to sterile, irrelevant tests guarantees a curriculum that will be as exciting as watching paint dry.

Focus on Process over Product

So the discussion has come full circle. If teachers expect students to be engaged and intrigued, then they need to do their part by carefully reexamining and then recrafting the curriculum so as to allow these goals to be achieved. Psychologist Jerome Bruner aptly said, "We teach a subject not to produce little living libraries on that subject, but rather to get a student to think mathematically for himself, to consider matters as an historian does, to take part in the process of knowledge-getting. Knowing is a process not a product" (Bruner 1966, 72).

The teacher may not be able to redirect students completely away from perfectionistic, solely product-driven work, but by rethinking the curriculum and questions posed to students, deeper thought can be encouraged and achieved. The renowned education psychologist Howard Gardner stated that the single greatest enemy to understanding is coverage (Brandt 1993). If teachers step beyond *coverage* of curriculum, then learning can become meaningful while embedding skills and concepts—not teaching in isolation.

Yes, teachers are responsible for successfully educating their students on concepts tied to their state standards. In many cases, job performance is primarily assessed on this issue. Regardless of the constraints, there are many things that you can do as a teacher to improve learning and engagement of your students. First, our attention needs to be focused on the process (the race) of learning and not become overly fixated on the product (the finish). When the process becomes central, then the final product should also improve. To begin to succeed with a student-centered, process-focused classroom, teachers need to constantly link learning to prior knowledge.

To begin shifting students from perfectionistic motives toward excellence first requires a paradigm shift in us as teachers. How you plan and then implement curriculum is critical. A good litmus test to evaluate your own teaching includes asking how often you make learning truly relevant for your students. Specifically, can you clearly answer why students need to know what you're teaching today? The latter issue of why today's lesson is important to know is where most get hung up. It is not sufficient to say they will need it for Algebra II next year or because it is on the state-mandated test.

Facilitate Meaningful Learning

So what can be done? One approach is to ask what are the eight to ten concepts or skills that you want your students to walk away with at the end of the year. Articulating these goals will then help to frame the curriculum. *Understanding by Design* (Wiggins and McTighe 1998) provides an excellent guide for helping teachers separate enduring knowledge from things that are just nice for students to be familiar with at the end of the course. Planning backward, endorsed by the Coalition of Essential Schools (McDonald 1992), is a similar idea that requires teachers to think about the end goal before developing the curriculum. Finally, essential questions (e.g., Who built America? What if everyone could see your thoughts? Are we what we eat?) provide an engaging framework to bring the unit or theme to life and also allow a place for key concepts to be integrated.

Once the enduring ideas are determined, the assignments and assessments need to be aligned to promote meaningful learning. While meaningful learning is clearly a truism, it is also much more. Originally, meaningful learning became important in attempting to distinguish learning that was not rote memorization. Today, it has a broader sense that includes the application and transference of knowledge. This use of knowledge requires that the learner is actively engaged in the learning process. A quick way to gauge the quality of learning that you are leading is to review your grade book. The grades you record are your way of emphasizing what is important to your students. If nothing else, your grades are intended to be a measure of the quality and degree of learning that has transpired in your class.

As you scan your grade book, consider what percentage of grades (1) are not knowledge-centered at all (e.g., completion, behavior, bringing materials to class), (2) require lower-order skills (e.g., define, list, name, recall—rote memorization), or (3) involve students in higher-order thinking (e.g., demonstrate, communicate, justify, transfer). When our students begin to engage in work that they see as meaningful and relevant to them, then we as teachers have a hope of facilitating the development of thinkers over fact- and algorithm-spewing automatons. The bottom line is: What expectations do you have for students that go beyond developing rote knowledge? If rote knowledge over deep conceptual understanding is preferred, then our jobs as teachers should be outsourced to computers in the years ahead. At least computers can quickly individualize instruction based on current ability and provide immediate feedback regarding performance.

Emphasize Ideas and Knowledge over Grades

In a recent conference on school restructuring, Ray McNulty, the executive director for the International Center for Leadership in Education, reminded participants that nationally only sixty-seven students out of one hundred who start their freshman year end up graduating from high school. Moreover, only eighteen out of one hundred starting high school freshmen will earn a college degree (McNulty 2005). Additionally, Robert Sternberg's *Successful Intelligence* reports that IQ only accounts for 10 percent of career success (1996). Both statistics serve to remind teachers and administrators that success is more dependent upon a mix of analytical knowledge (critical thinking skills), practical knowledge (application of knowledge), and creative knowledge (innovative ideas), and not just content mastery. At present, most academic programs have poor alignment between life and school.

Most Overachievers tend to place importance on grades and not on learning. They achieve an A on an exam or project but forget the content within days because they never truly learned it in the first place. When an Overachiever is anxious about a grade, let them know that grades are merely *one* way of gauging how much they have learned. Although you may not want to admit it to the students, grades are often a poor indicator of what was actually learned. Specifically, a grade can be very precise (e.g., 89.25 percent) but be highly invalid (e.g. an A often does not indicate excellent, profound learning, or even understanding of the key objectives). Furthermore, if we are only measuring trivial things that do not relate to the students' prior knowledge, then the measuring stick is highly flawed.

Remember that assessment measures are only as valid as the rubric being used. Rubrics can be made for anything, but does the rubric capture and emphasize the essence of knowledge and understanding desired? Or does the rubric emphasize extraneous yet measurable things such as format, length, syntax (in a non-writing course), or attractiveness?

Since Overachievers tend to become overly grade-focused, encouraging them to participate in class discussions and cooperative learning situations allows them to develop their often lagging interpersonal skills. If they are upset about a grade, suggest that they *delve deeper* within the content and redo part of an assignment to ensure that they understand the content and find the *missing pieces*. Overachievers frequently assume there is only one correct answer. They know how to maneuver from Point A to Point B and are satisfied when Point B is reached. Overachievers, however, rarely want to learn different ways to reach the end point or the solution to a problem. Encourage an Overachiever to look at a problem or question from multiple perspectives.

Also, by responding to more open-ended, higher-order questioning prompts for discussions and assignments, students will begin thinking about responses instead of merely filling in empty spaces on worksheets.

Provide Assessments to Encourage Deeper Thinking

Several things can be done to address the perfectionism issue. For instance, when developing a rubric to go along with an assignment, like an essay in English or a presentation in social studies, make the top marking for mastery a B instead of the usual A. Thus, complete, competent mastery denotes a B performance. Then leave space on the rubric for value added. You likely have read many essays that are complete and meet the rubric but still do not denote excellence. It will then be up to the individual student to justify why and where the work demonstrates excellence or A work.

These value-added rubrics serve two purposes. First, they engage the student in the evaluation process—instead of making it something done to the student. Thus, self-knowledge is developed that encourages lifelong learning. Plus, creativity and knowledge can all be celebrated in the same assignment. Students entrenched in the old system are likely to squawk at this system at first, but with patience and time, self-learning can be fostered. Furthermore, making most assessments formative instead of summative encourages students to continue honing their work.

Be forewarned that change will not always be received favorably. Be patient. Be consistent. Be persistent. Rewards should begin to show in time. The teacher, or department, will need to address the more subtle issues where incredible value has been added but the work lacks demonstration of mastery of all essential ideas or skills. Is this a B or must it be reworked and then resubmitted? Remember the goal of grades should not be seen as punishment. Rather, it should provide a clear indicator of a student's current level of ability.

REFERENCES

Brandt, R. (1993). On teaching for understanding: A conversation with Howard Gardner. *Education Leadership 50*(7): 4–7.

Bruner, J. S. (1966). *Toward a theory of instruction.* Cambridge, MA: Belknap Press.

Littky, D. (2004). *The big picture: Education is everyone's business.* Alexandria, VA: ASCD.

McDonald, J. (1992). Steps in planning backwards: Early lessons from the schools [electronic version]. *CES National Web.* www.essentialschools.org/cs/resources/view/ces_res/121 (accessed June 3, 2006).

McNulty, R. (2005). Lessons learned in secondary schools. cell.uindy.edu/clearing house/mcnulty_powerpoint.pdf (accessed June 20, 2006).

Meier, D. (1995). *The power of their ideas.* Boston: Beacon Press.

Sizer, T. R. (1992). *Horace's school: Redesigning the American high school.* Boston: Houghton Mifflin.

Sternberg, R. J. (1996). *Successful intelligence: How practical and creative intelligence determining success in life.* New York: Plume.

Wiggins, G., and McTighe, J. (1998). *Understanding by design.* Alexandria, VA: ASCD.

CHAPTER 5

The Player
December 14

J. B. Harris towers over his teachers and classmates and assumes the role of the popular athlete. He slides by with his grades, so as to maintain eligibility. To Players like J. B., school is merely another drill the coaches say is necessary for success. The Player can be the school politician, the class clown, or the star athlete. In this chapter, J. B. discovers his game plan is not without fault.

Mrs. Maccabee hustles through the hallway with her arms full of leftover cookies from the National Honor Society's monthly meeting. In her mind, she replays the final moments of her twelve-year-old son Cory's first indoor soccer game from the night before. As her face twists into a smile, recalling the goal he saved, the booming voice of Bob Brown startles her.

"Maccabee, the school needs your help."

Slightly confused, but curious nonetheless, Mrs. Maccabee sets down her cookie platter on an empty desk in the hallway and turns her attention to the young coach.

"J. B. Harris, my starting center, seems to be having some trouble in your class. He's a really talented kid, and the school needs him this year. With the failing grade in your class, though, I'm afraid he won't be eligible this season," Coach Brown explains in his salesman voice. "Now, don't get me wrong, I'm not asking for anything unfair. I just thought that a nice teacher like you could assist our basketball star," continues Brown. Without waiting for a response, he turns away with a smile. "I'll come by your room later this week to see if we can work out a game plan."

> Is it ever appropriate to provide extra assistance for students because of their involvement in sports or other school activities?

J. B. Harris strolls into second period fifteen seconds after the bell rings, making no attempt to hurry. Ignoring the frown from his teacher, he plops down into the far-right desk in the second row. J. B. looks more ready for a basketball game than geometry, wearing Air Jordans and a Timberwolves jersey. He carries a bottle of orange juice in one hand and notebook in the other, and as the other students open their notebooks, he pulls a Snickers Marathon bar from his pocket. Students like J. B. were not considered when student desks were invented; his head peaks above the others, and his legs sprawl out to make room under the desk. He constantly shifts position and attempts to stretch, from a combination of boredom and discomfort.

Mrs. Maccabee is perched on a stool at the front of the classroom, with a textbook across her lap. As she displays and reads overhead transparencies from the last textbook adoption, she writes in hints and shortcuts with her favorite blue marker, a color she always uses to show her school spirit. The students in her geometry class span a large range of aptitudes and ages. Furthermore, an outsider would quickly notice the varying levels of engagement. In front of J. B. sits Emi, a bright student who recently moved from a much smaller school several hours to the south. Emi takes copious notes and often stays after class to ask questions. J. B. uses his height, even when sitting, to his advantage. He does not take notes and only glances at the overhead screen a few times during class, but he resourcefully uses a borrowed pencil from Emi to unsuspectingly copy her answers to the homework.

> How should the teacher respond when he or she notices that a student is copying a homework assignment, quiz, or test?

When the bell rings he springs from his seat, puts Emi's pencil in his pocket, and hands Mrs. Maccabee his half-completed homework. She protests, but he mutters that he would not finish it anyway so she might as well take it. Mrs. Maccabee holds the paper for a few seconds and then walks to her computer. At least he is trying, she thinks. She remembers his older brothers, troublemakers who flunked off the basketball team and never graduated. As she looks across J. B.'s row in the grade book, she sees that at least he usually turns in something, even if it is rarely complete.

Maybe I've been too hard on him, not giving him credit for his effort, she thinks. She questions herself, *Have I been after him to turn in extra credit? I did talk to his mother about his grade, and after that he turned in some late work.* With the school's emphasis on decreasing student failure, Mrs. Maccabee worries that she could have done more to help J. B. *Without basketball, he would be lost, and without him the team will suffer,* she thinks as she adds a few percentage points here and there. Although feeling uneasy, she resolves that tomorrow she will talk with him after class about his effort.

Where does teacher responsibility end? Student responsibility?

J. B. finds a few teammates in the hallway, and his sullen classroom demeanor disappears as he begins good-natured teasing with the guys and flirting with the girls in his group. J. B.'s friends attract attention in the halls; the guys are either taller or more muscular than their peers, dressed in baggy athletic gear. The girls are good-looking, all either perky cheerleaders or fit athletes. J. B.'s group is diverse, with a mix of races, socioeconomics, and even grades; the uniting factor is success in sports. J. B. strolls through the hall, as if he has no reason to hurry and slides into Coach Wright's class just as the bell rings. Although a coach's class is often an athlete's favorite, J. B. detests the coach as a teacher.

"He's always blabbering on in his big voice about something or another. And his jokes—they're the worst. If there's a football game, he always gives us time to work in class. But forget it during basketball season," J. B. complained to his mother the last time grades came out. As usual, J. B.'s mom told him to stop whining.

She says, "Life isn't always fair. You're going to have to learn to work for people you don't like." Needless to say, his grade was not above the passing mark in this class either.

Toward the end of the period, Bob Brown appears at the door and looks in. Coach Wright has just wrapped up his lecture and is giving homework questions from the book when Brown asks, "Do you have a minute?"

In the hallway Brown gives his coaching buddy a smile and apologizes for coming during class time. Brown and Wright respect one another as coaches and individuals, but also feel the slight competitive edge of leading the two large sports programs. Many of the top athletes could play either basketball or football, but both coaches encourage only one sport. Also, the two teams compete for booster money and bragging rights as the best school sport. Brown is fairly confident, however, that Wright will be sympathetic toward his center.

Brown gives the same spiel as with Mrs. Maccabee. The only difference being that his salesman tone is replaced with an I'm-sure-you-understand tone. Before Coach Wright can respond, Brown winks and leaves him. Coach Wright stands just inside the door of his own classroom, with a stern expression. He watches J. B.

Slumped down in his chair, J. B. writes answers quickly, without even looking in the book. He turns to the junior class secretary, seated to his left, and asks for one of the answers. She tries to talk through her answer but finally hands over her paper. J. B. writes noticeably shorter responses to a couple questions and hands it back. He glances at his watch, rips the paper out of his notebook, and stretches out in his seat. Clearly, he has checked out for the period.

> Do the benefits of providing time to complete homework during class outweigh the negatives, such as students not using their time?

Because he doesn't think the coach ever pays any attention to his students during the work time at the end of each period, J. B. thinks he can discreetly slip his iPod headphones into his ears. The iPod was his only birthday gift, a joint effort from his mother, grandmother, and aunt last year. He keeps it with him at all times, waiting for an unobservant teacher to give him the chance to escape the class.

I'm so tired of this stupid schoolwork. We've seriously been studying the Civil War since like third grade. Reading the textbook every day isn't going to change anything about the future anyway, J. B. thinks to himself, in rhythm with music. *I wonder what Coach was talking to Wright about anyway. Too bad Coach says he can't get me out of this class. Wright's been hard on me ever since I quit playing football freshman year.*

Watching J. B. angers Coach Wright. *His story is no different than anyone else's*, Wright thinks to himself. Wright had both of J. B.'s older brothers in class, and they both dropped out before graduation. He feels safe in assuming that they have held a string of menial jobs and probably have a few kids by now. *J. B. is lazy and will turn out just like his brothers, and there is nothing I am going to do about it*, he resolves. *Just because he's tall and quick, basketball comes easy to him; he tries to approach school the same way, and this is one class where he cannot just play the game to get a D.*

It's 3:00, and the hallways fill with the chaos of another day completed. J. B. chats with Tina Hodges as he makes his way toward the gym for practice. She always knows what's happening over the weekend, and even though she is not J. B.'s type, he enjoys having the attention of a Socialite. As he enters the locker room, he laughs to himself at the thought of taking Tina to the Christmas dance, just to see what people would think. Tina is not a part of his typical group, but she always makes an appearance at his buddies' parties. He decides that he will stop by the party at her friend Sam's house this weekend.

As J. B. and his teammates start to warm up, Coach Brown appears at the door of gym and motions for J. B. "We need to talk for a minute," Brown tells him, with a serious tone. "Your grades are not good, not good at all, J. B. Why do we have this trouble every season? I can get you a tutor if that would help, but I'm sensing the problem is more about work ethic though."

> How can teachers encourage students to see the importance of education, beyond just academic eligibility?

J. B. averts his eyes and says, "Nah, Coach. I'll be okay."

"I'm not sure yet if all your teachers have their final grades figured, but the grades I've seen do not qualify you for basketball, at least until Christmas. I've talked to your teachers, but I need your help here. Show them that you care, and that might make a difference. Now get out there and get ready to work on your post moves."

"All right, Coach."

J. B. has a good practice, pulling down numerous rebounds during the scrimmage. When they are shooting free throws at the end, though, he starts to worry about his grades. Every season his coaches get worried about his grades. Then, J. B. copies a little extra credit or actually takes his homework home for a day or two. He is thinking about Coach Wright's class, though. *Other guys on the team don't fail his class like I do*, he thinks, recalling the locker room discussions about boring teachers. *Is he out to get me? Or have I been slacking too much?* J. B. sinks his final free throw and heads to the locker room, distracted by his teammates' talk of the upcoming weekend.

Before he leaves the gym, Bob Brown sends an e-mail to Mrs. Maccabee and Coach Wright, inviting both of them to a holiday dinner party at his house. The e-mail mentions nothing about his earlier discussions, but the last line reads, "My team and I know we can always count on your school spirit."

> What are some ways to maintain professionalism and strong ethical beliefs while retaining friendships with coworkers?

Giving the situation more thought, he decides to call Linda Morrow, J. B.'s mother. Linda is accustomed to these phone calls, right before grades come out. Despite her determination during their previous conversations, her older two sons still flunked off the team, gave up on the sport, and then dropped out of school. Since J. B. is the only one left at home, Coach Brown thinks she might have a chance to make a difference this time.

Coach Brown has always liked Linda, and he realizes she certainly has her hands full. *It must be tough to raise three boys*, he thinks, *especially ones as stubborn as those Harris kids are*. From what he knew, Linda had been married until J. B. was about two. She made jokes that her boys had run off every man whom she'd ever brought home. Brown knew that she often worked overtime, which usually meant she was not home when J. B. was done with practice. However, he remembers from an earlier conversation that this is her evening off.

Linda is not surprised to hear the coach's voice on the other end of the phone; she has just asked J. B. about his grades and knows they are probably not as "okay" as he insisted. Feeling both frustrated and disappointed, Linda finally asks the coach what she must be doing wrong as a parent. "I just don't know how other single moms do it," she explains. "J. B. doesn't get in trouble like his brothers did, and no teachers have called lately. His math teacher called several weeks ago, but he told me that he turned in some late work and raised his grade. He's not a bad kid, but he just doesn't care about school. And I'm so tired all the time and work so late . . ." and with a sigh, her voice trails off.

Bob Brown assures her that he will do his part to keep on top of the grades too. He decides to set J. B. up with a daily report system, requiring each teacher to initial and record any missing work. He also suggests that she try contacting one teacher per week to check on his progress. By the end of the phone call, her voice calms, and they talk about the season.

> What are effective ways to foster strong parent-teacher relationships?

After he hangs up the phone, Bob wonders if J. B. will be able to play after grades come out. He is confident that he can get J. B.'s grades up, but it might be too late for this progress report. *If only he had checked the grades sooner; if only J.B. had the much easier Mrs. Harper for history; if only kids cared about school like they used to*, he reflects on all the possibilities as he drives home for the evening.

INTERACTING WITH THE PLAYER

Student athletes, thespians, and musicians are accustomed to putting in great amounts of effort to achieve the desired success or victory at the game, show, or competition. If these students are provided strong leadership during their training, they typically improve their individual performance as well as their contribution to the team or group. This effort when coupled with perseverance can overcome many obstacles that stand between the student and success in the classroom. Additionally, the strategies that we employ in the classroom to engage and facilitate student learning are critical for success and overall academic achievement.

Increase Effort

When the Player raises the level of effort devoted to learning, the results should be quickly noticeable to both the teacher and student. Increasing effort is not the same as just awarding credit each time a student fills out a worksheet. When teachers give reasons why students should expend effort, students tend to be much more receptive and often are willing to *buy in*.

For instance, a typical assignment might ask students to write a well-crafted paragraph that includes at least two supporting ideas and five sentences, but the reason to make the effort is missing. The reason might be as simple as this is the minimum standard for you to demonstrate that you can logically link ideas together. Or this assignment is very important because once you can do this well, you will be more effective in writing essays, letters, or other assignments. Moreover, success with this skill will help you in all your courses and throughout life. Effective communicators will be more likely to excel in their careers. So how do we successfully encourage those who are resistant to beginning their assignments?

Teachers often create behavioral contracts with students. This same principle can be applied to the concept of effort. Why not write a contract with a Player to increase the level of effort given in class? This contract can include the effort made to take notes and organize information provided in class (this likely will need some clear guidance at first). Programs such as AVID or Cornell notes are great examples of helping to provide students with a structure for how to organize information in more meaningful ways. The contract might include listing the goal related to effort, stating obstacles that could distract the student from achieving the goal, detailing where assistance can be found, and describing the consequences if the contract is broken (Mendler 2000).

So the first goal is to get the students engaged in meaningful learning experiences. Effort is a great initial step that should produce nice results, but this effort will only show lasting results if it is accompanied with persistence. With a little cajoling, we can get students to put forward some effort, but if perseverance is lacking, then success will be minimal at best. Students who lack perseverance show increasingly sparse note taking as the year proceeds, or they listen to the directions for a major project but then neglect to complete the assignment. Likewise, when effort dwindles, the final assignment submitted is either incomplete or missing altogether.

Very few students lack the desire to succeed in school. If you poll students, most aspire to earn a high grade in your course at the beginning of the school year. Moreover, they will acknowledge how important it is to give sufficient effort to achieve this goal. However, within a matter of a few days, students like the Player quickly lose the perseverance necessary to achieve academic success; yet they will willingly practice the same drill on a basketball court or on a stage until mastery and confidence have been achieved. The difference is that the Player has taken ownership in pursuing the goals and sees personal relevance in the endeavor being pursued.

How students perceive our classrooms and thus decide to persevere or not is partially under our control. We must make the standards come alive for students. Most students, including the Player, are not interested in irrelevant exercises, such as "This is important because it will be on your test next Friday." Mathematics teachers may struggle with this idea more than other disciplines.

Students are not impressed when they are told this is important because it will be used in geometry next year or because we will use it in the next section to solve similar problems. Make it relevant now! To expect students to excel, we need to be equipped to do better as teachers in providing valuable motivation. That may mean that we need to be better salespeople. If you cannot convince yourself of the importance of particular content, then visit with your colleagues to develop a plan. If you are not convinced of the importance, then your students will not be either.

Refuse to Play the Game of Minimalism

Students like J. B. approach school as a game where winning is just passing, rather than learning. It is unreasonable for teachers to think that all students will excel in our classes, but it *is* reasonable to expect a high level of competency from all students. To best prepare the Player for life, teachers should keep expectations high. When we accept incomplete work or just let students copy work from another student, then we become a player in a game that enables student failure. Life after high school will not be so kind, and few jobs will tolerate workers who regularly leave tasks unfinished. Set high yet attainable expectations early and communicate these with students. Consider including on your first-day handout that incomplete work will not be accepted. When asking students to work in groups, give each student an accountability piece and demonstrate that copying answers is not acceptable by requiring students to redo these assignments.

Find the Motivator

Whether the Player is an athlete or not, something outside of education often motivates her to pass her academic classes. Developing a relationship with your students will provide insight into the positive influences in their lives. Introductory activities during the first weeks of school or journal writing can reveal students' motivating factors. Once you can pinpoint what motivates a student, try to use it to your advantage.

J. B.'s teachers know that basketball is the motivator, and they can use Coach Brown as an ally. Going further, include texts in your content area that relate to these interests or give choices that allow students to bring in their interests. Any activity that bridges the gap between school and the outside interests can encourage relevant learning. For some students, the outside motivator may be difficult to pinpoint, but for the Player, the motivator is clear—good grades so a scholarship in the area of talent can be earned or in more severe cases so eligibility can continue.

When teaching star students such as J. B., seek to broaden your relationship to include the area of greatest talent plus other lesser-known interests. Although asking about the game or performance will help build rapport, discussing additional topics will remind the Player that she is multidimensional. Activities such as student learning inventories may help bring out other aspects of the students' personality to explore and will also aid in grouping students. Students, community members, and other staff already feed the Player's ego; in your class, make sure all students are learners first and foremost, thus not overemphasizing their well-known accomplishments.

Sometimes it is possible to connect students with role models in the community. Although it is often difficult for the Player to see beyond their area of passion, we owe it to our students to show them what life after school looks like. A select few will make it as professional athletes or performers, so while teachers can encourage the pursuit of their primary interest, we should also help students see all the options that might be available to them. In essence, teachers can help build options for students. Having former star athletes, musicians, artists, or thespians come back and talk about how they are successful in other areas provides a good insight into the future.

Less than 1 percent of college athletes (even lower for high school athletes) become professionals in their sport. So the goal is not to squash dreams and areas of passion but, rather, to prepare students for life. Having multiple options is good for all students, not just the Player. If the trend remains, today's youth will have approximately five different careers in their lifetime. Thus, flexibility and adaptability are critical.

Vary Instructional Strategies

Encouraging effort, keeping standards high, and identifying the motivator for the Player are all important, but these are mostly external processes that assist instruction and learning. The final strategy focuses on instructional practice. A key component of effective instruction necessitates providing variety in the instructional techniques used to guide learning. Variety is vital, but it is important to be clear on the rationale for why to vary instruction. Howard Gardner focuses on the multiple intelligences of learners; variety and choice are essential components of instruction so that the needs of all learners are met. For instance, some are kinesthetic, some are musical, and some are verbal in their primary intelligence. Thus, we need to make sure their intelligence is celebrated in the way that we teach and learn (Gardner 1983).

Since Players often learn well in an interactive setting, lecture, for these students, should be engaging if possible and minimized time-wise. For instance, direct or lecture instruction should be used to (1) explicitly address misconceptions, (2) unite student ideas together into the context of past, present, and future learning, and (3) assist in providing further examples and applications of the knowledge. Contrarily, lecture should be avoided as a means to cover material and produce a tome of information to study for the ensuing exam. This emphasis toward finding better ways to engage the learner while minimizing teacher-directed learning is good for promoting deeper understanding in students such as the Player, the Underachiever, and the Socialite. This trend toward student-centered learning is more appropriate in today's society where information is abundant and critical thinking is required.

How People Learn (National Research Council 2000) provides evidence that higher student achievement occurs when students are first given a period of time to work with new concepts and ideas in an engaging way and then are provided with a summative lecture to pull information together. This finding emphasizes that limiting lecture time is important, but so too is the timing of the lecture in relation to learning activities. Specifically, lectures have a powerful effect when they follow a period of student exploration—not when they precede it.

The Player shares many overlapping tendencies with other archetypes. For instance, many Players are also Socialites and focus on their interpersonal skills to carry them academically. The Player also shares many common characteristics with the Overwhelmed and the Downtrodden, which will be discussed in the chapters that follow. The Player is unique from all the other archetypes in that these students possess an amazing talent in one area but lack the desire or ability to transfer the skills and aptitude in their forte to their academic performance.

REFERENCES

Gardner, H. (1983). *Frames of mind: The theory of multiple intelligences*. New York: Basic Books.

Mendler, A. N. (2000). *Motivating students who don't care: Successful techniques for educators*. Bloomington, IN: Solution Tree.

National Research Council. (2000). *How people learn*. Washington, DC: National Academy Press.

CHAPTER 6

The Overwhelmed

January 30

Emi Choi transferred to Roosevelt High School from a smaller, more suburban setting. She can be seen diligently taking notes and rechecking her assignments in class, always questioning her abilities. Like other Overwhelmed students, Emi seems lost in her large school—a little scared, often lonely, and under pressure from herself and her parents. In this chapter, starting a new semester leads Emi to even higher levels of stress and anxiety, and she needs someone to notice her struggles.

Señora Hernandez's day begins before most of her students get out of bed. As department chair and head of numerous committees, there rarely is a day on her calendar without a meeting or other obligation. She regularly arrives at school by 6 a.m., and today is no exception. After a textbook adoption committee meeting and an encouraging conversation with a first-year Spanish teacher, Esperanza Hernandez begins redecorating a portion of her classroom with colorful posters and collages from her second-year students.

> How can schools better distribute nonacademic assignments so that the same teachers are not called on for every task?

To outside observers, her classroom always assumes the atmosphere of a Mexican fiesta—colorful décor, music playing, and food every Friday. As she sings along to her favorite CD, she does not notice the timid, petite student enter her room. Emi Choi stands in the doorway and apprehensively knocks, but to no avail. She carries a large tray covered in plastic wrap. After a few moments, she gingerly approaches her teacher from behind and taps her on the shoulder.

After a brief startle, Señora Hernandez greets Emi, "¡Hola, señorita! Buenos días. You are here early this morning."

"Um, Señora, I brought my food," Emi says as she places the heaping tray of Mexican wedding cakes on the table designated for her class.

"Gracias! They look delicious." Señora Hernandez learned years ago that her students considered "Señora" her name, and she decided she had bigger issues than requiring them to call her by her correct name. Throughout the school, she was known simply as Señora to both students and teachers.

"Thank you," Emi says politely. "Could I . . . talk to you for a minute?"

Señora Hernandez motions for Emi to have a seat as she turns down her music. She pulls up a student desk to face Emi. "What can I do for you?"

Emi opens her bulging backpack, placing a large, neatly labeled Español 2 binder on the desk. She opens to the syllabus on the first page, and Señora Hernandez immediately notices that nearly everything on the page is highlighted. Emi says quietly, "Señora, I think this class might be too much for me." She points to items on the page. "So many projects. And quizzes. It takes me longer to learn the words than everyone else, I think. Is there a different class I could take, or a different language maybe? I'm just not sure that I'm going to do well."

"Emi, don't be discouraged! You are a very bright girl, and such a hard worker. I could set you up with a tutor if you would like." Señora Hernandez pats Emi's hand and smiles encouragingly.

"I make notecards for all the words, and I write down everything you say in class. It's just so much information though. Whenever I start a test, it all just jumbles together."

"A new language is always challenging. It sounds like you are doing the right things as you study. Maybe you can study with a friend. That always helped me when I was a student."

"I, I guess, maybe." Emi nods her head, as if to convince herself.

Then the warning bell rings, signaling that classes start in five minutes. Emi politely thanks Señora Hernandez and leaves the room. The frenetic pace of the day is now in full swing, as students begin entering the classroom and two teachers appear in the doorway with questions for her as department chair.

Emi Choi has few friends. She still considers herself the *new kid* despite starting her second semester at Roosevelt High. In English, her first-period class, there is only one other student whom she talks to, but this student is absent today. She gets to work immediately on her *Of Mice and Men* test. As usual, other students finish while she is less than half done. As Miss Smith gives a time reminder, only ten minutes left, Emi feels her heart start to race as she looks at the remaining essay question.

Feeling defeated, she barely speaks to her best friend, Amy, as they walk to second period. Amy is busy telling a story about her new crush, and doesn't seem to notice Emi's downfallen attitude.

As Amy giggles and rambles, Emi continues to think through the questions on the English test. *I studied for thirty minutes last night, and I reread the end of the book over the weekend*, she thinks to herself. *I highlighted quotes on every page and read over them again and again.*

In the standards-based classroom, how can teachers effectively incorporate study skills and time management techniques?

Emi sits uncomfortably in Mrs. Maccabee's geometry class. The huge basketball player sits behind her again this semester because Mrs. Maccabee decided not to change the seating arrangement. Emi sits erectly, feeling the eyes of J. B. Harris on her assignments, his legs poking out on either side of her desk. She feels so small and unknown compared to J. B., especially in the hallway. Her locker is next to his, and he never acknowledges her existence, and usually blocks her path.

Emi can barely concentrate on the lecture, her mind turning over the upcoming assignments in all of her classes. *Math homework, study for Tuesday's math quiz; science lab write-up and extra credit.* . . . At the end of the period, Mrs. Maccabee passes back last week's quizzes.

78%—C is written in Mrs. Maccabee's signature Roosevelt-blue marker across the top of her quiz. Emi clenches her face muscles, waging war with her watery eyes. "I will not cry in class," she repeats to herself firmly over and over.

She makes her way to her third-period health class, not even paying attention to her surroundings. She continues to think how upset her father will be when he asks about her recent math quiz. In health class she is working on a group project on tobacco awareness. Although the assignment is considered a *group project*, Emi single-handedly creates the poster for her group while the three other students joke around about the weekend and pretend to highlight information when the teacher walks by. At the end of the period, only Ivory stays to help her clean up, mostly so he can see his girlfriend entering for the next class period. "Looks like you'll have to finish it over the weekend," he mutters as he leaves the class.

> What can teachers do to encourage individual accountability on group assignments? How can unequal work be addressed for group projects?

Amy is worried when Emi does not meet her for lunch, but she would have been even more shocked to learn that Emi had skipped her fourth-period class. Emi has achieved perfect attendance for the past three years, even coming to school with strep throat during first semester. Emi sits in a bathroom stall, clenching a notebook to her chest, rocking back and forth. Tears stream down her smooth face. She breathes in little gasps, staring straight ahead at the blank stall door. When she hears the voices of Tina Hodges and her friends gossiping while fixing their hair, she carefully holds her breath.

Finally Emi opens her journal. She began journaling upon a suggestion from her English teacher in eighth grade as a way to relieve stress. As she wipes her face with a little wad of toilet paper, she begins to write slowly and deliberately at first and then builds up speed.

I hate this school. This big school. No one knows me. They aren't even sure I can speak English. They don't know where I came from, and I miss my friends—Julie, Morgan, Leah, and Beth. We did things on weekends. Then my dad lost his job, and we had to move. Now I always study. I have to go to college, my dad says. We can't afford college, so I have to get scholarships. My grades aren't good enough. What is wrong with me, my dad asks. Don't I care about the sacrifices he makes? I work harder and harder, and I do worse and worse. So many projects this semester. And I do badly on all the quizzes. I see other kids hanging out with their girlfriends or boyfriends, going to movies on the weekends, and attending sports and dances. They are so much happier than me. People know them. No one knows me. Why do I try? Why do I care? It just gets harder, and I get nothing for it. I can't get straight As, and my dad will punish me unless I do. It's just not worth it anymore. I quit.

How can students be helped during transitions to new schools or new learning environments?

Señora Hernandez buzzes with energy—clapping, chanting, and cheering her way through the school day. She begins her second-year Spanish class with a sing-along to a festive winter song to liven up her lesson on verb tenses and weather words. After a fast-paced review, in which students eagerly raise their hands to earn stickers on their participation log, it is time to share food. Each student introduces his or her food, and then passes it around the room. Emi speaks so softly that no one even hears her brief introduction, "Mexican wedding cakes. They're cookies." The food is gobbled down quickly with fiesta music playing in the background.

After a sixty-second clean-up, which the students are accustomed to, Señora posts the instructions for a two-day group project. Students already know their assigned teams. They are the same teams they have worked with throughout the first month of the semester.

As she circulates around the room, checking on groups and answering questions, Señora Hernandez remembers her morning conversation with Emi. She watches Emi's group for a moment; Emi sits sullenly, staring blankly at the board while the other three girls in her group giggle through the brainstorming session. Señora Hernandez approaches Emi, placing her hand on her shoulder. "¿Como estás, senorita?"

Emi looks up quickly and mumbles "Bien" behind her hand.

Before she has a chance to question her further, another student summons Señora's attention from across the room. Time goes so fast in Señora Hernandez's world! She can't believe it when the bell rings to release the class. As the students rush out the door, Señora catches up with Emi. "Can you stay a second, Emi? We didn't get to finish our talk from this morning."

Emi stares at her, shaking her head. "Never mind. I, uh, I'll figure it out."

"I'm sure you will!" Señora Hernandez reassures her. Then Emi slips away from Señora as two junior class officers begin busily asking Señora Hernandez prom questions.

> How can teachers effectively juggle different responsibilities while not sacrificing instructional quality?

At the end of the day, Emi unloads the contents of her backpack into her locker, taking only her journal home. She leaves her homework unfinished, her tests not studied for. Emi has entered the world of apathy, and no one knows.

INTERACTING WITH THE OVERWHELMED

School for many of our students becomes an overpowering series of interwoven stimuli. In a typical day, the need to successfully organize and then succeed in six classes becomes too much. The Overwhelmed often becomes frantic, frustrated, and forgetful. To an observer, this frantic behavior may seem silly, but the feelings are very real to the Overwhelmed student.

Break Down Assignments

The first day or two of school is often a bit overwhelming for everyone as a comprehensive view of the semester is presented. For most these feelings quickly subside, and their efforts quickly transition to focusing on individual assignments as they come. However, the Overwhelmed sees a syllabus or major assignment, and immediately feels anxious over trying to remember all the expectations and details of each assignment. To help the Overwhelmed, it is important to remind students that the syllabus or overview of a major assignment is just for the purpose of generating a road map.

After an overview has been provided, then assignments need to be broken into smaller, more manageable chunks. Although Señora Hernandez appropriately prepares her students for the semester with her syllabus, a student like Emi fails to see that these assignments are spread out and manageable. In *A Framework for Understanding Poverty*, Ruby Payne includes this chunking strategy as an effective technique for improving student success. All students, not just the Overwhelmed, will benefit from being taught this process. Breaking down assignments also allows teachers to troubleshoot by monitoring students' understanding and progress along the way. Clearly breaking the components of the assignment down *with* the students, not *for* the student, builds an effective roadmap for students to navigate.

Find Flow

Part of the art of teaching is knowing when and how to challenge students properly. When students are not challenged enough, they become overly relaxed and bored. On the other hand, if teachers provide too great a challenge for students, then students become frustrated. If great enough, this frustration will lead to anxiety and feelings of being overwhelmed. When an optimal balance has been achieved, where the level of skill matches the level of challenge, then one can experience what Csikszentmihalyi (1997) calls flow. So balancing the level of rigor that students are exposed to can encourage flow or feelings of "being in the zone."

Athletes and performers often experience flow when they maximally execute their skill in a challenging setting. However, a novice chess player does not experience flow when playing a chess master because the level of challenge is too high for the current skill level. Likewise, the typical eighth grade student would not feel flow if placed in an advanced calculus class because his or her skill is too low with respect to the challenge. This same feeling of being underprepared for the task is experienced by many students when then walk into their classes daily. When students lack the key skills necessary to organize, understand, master, or apply the concepts being studied, they will experience a sense of being overwhelmed.

Students will not feel great levels of achievement or flow if the long-term solution is to lower the expectations. Instead, the teacher should make every effort to keep the level of challenge high but continue to build the skill level so that success can be realized and celebrated. One indicator of flow is a distorted sense of time. Most have experienced a meeting or class that seemed to drone on for days. This is a distorted sense of time but in the wrong direction. Instead, do your students comment as they leave class, "Where did the time go?" This and similar comments provide one indicator that some or all students experienced the positive sensation of flow during that class period.

A few things that assist promoting flow include having clear goals and objectives, balancing skill level with challenge level, linking learning to students' lives, and providing relevant, quick feedback. Athletes often have immediate feedback regarding their performance (e.g., an assist led to a score). In the classroom, feedback is often days or weeks behind when the performance occurred, so if feedback becomes more immediate, then students become more vested in the process. The implementation of peer editing is one of many effective ways to make feedback more immediate. Remember, just because you experience flow as a teacher does not mean that the students are experiencing the same thing.

When the curriculum becomes more engaging and student-centered, then more opportunities for flow exist. Assignments or investigations that encourage students to question, explore, observe, and explain the world around them—such as inquiry-based or problem-based learning—encourage flow. Teacher-centered learning, where the learner must come through the teacher before learning can take place, tends to inhibit flow because students typically are not highly challenged or are poorly engaged. The other extreme where students are asked to engage in poorly structured inquiry can have the opposite problem of presenting too great a challenge for the skill level of the student.

A balance is achieved during guided inquiry experiences where the teacher helps to frame the content and broader question being studied. Then, students are encouraged to develop a method for studying the phenomenon. The teacher can scaffold learning by providing greater assistance to groups who are confused about how to proceed—thus keeping the level of challenge in line with the current skill level. For individuals or groups who are more able, they can be encouraged to tackle a more challenging aspect of the problem.

Essential questions that explore "Whose history is it?" or "Are you what you eat?" provide a rich array of ways for students to learn key standards or concepts in a way that fits their skill level. As teachers we need to find ways to better embed the mundane into more thought-provoking learning experiences. Students do not come to class excited to learn about meiosis or Shakespeare, but they are intrigued by why they have blue eyes when their parents have brown eyes or by how famous quotes become part of today's culture through music, art, and conversation.

Slow It Down—Encourage Metacognitive Reflection

In our frenetically paced world where rapid coverage of material is the norm, we can easily forget the primary goal of education—student learning. Over the past two decades enormous strides have been made in brain-based research that helps provide insights into how we learn in various situations. One of the areas receiving considerable attention is metacognition—thinking about our own thinking. Initial research on metacognition focused largely on adult populations, but now we see the positive effects that incorporating metacognitive reflection into the classroom can have on student learning.

When students personally become attuned to what they know and how they know it, they begin to take charge of their own learning. For instance, the use of science notebooks or student journals has been shown to improve metacognitive abilities of students (Shepardson and Britsch 2001). When students begin to take ownership of their learning, then the long-term impact will be lifelong learning. The short-term effect will be a difference in the way students perform and behave in class.

For instance, you should see fewer questions like, "I understood it when you did it in class, but then it didn't make sense when I tried it at home." These questions should begin to give way to "I understand the first two steps in the solution, but I am confused why you inverted and then multiplied during step three." Better still, it is exciting when students begin to be confident in exploring alternative solution paths: "My approach to solving the problem was very different, yet my reasoning and final answer still appear correct."

Reduce Cognitive Load

The final strategy involves helping students remove or reduce that which clutters thinking. When we first learn something new, we become hypervigilant to every stimulus that confronts us. Just think about the first time you learned to drive (particularly if it was a manual transmission). You had to apply the right amount of acceleration, let the clutch out in a smooth fashion, watch both ways, be aware of others on the road, consider where your hands were on the steering wheel, remember and apply the two-second rule, turn your blinker on at the appropriate time, and the list goes on. Now, most all of these things have been overlearned, which allows you to attend to other things. When we overlearn, we lower the cognitive load needed to attend to basic concepts. This allows greater attention to be given to more complex ideas.

Specifically, if a student knows key vocabulary in a foreign language class, multiplication tables in a math class, or symbols of common elements in a chemistry class, then they are able to concentrate respectively on conversations, problem-solving, or chemical reactions with much greater acuity. The key resides in how the cognitive load for basic skills is reduced. For students who wrestle with basic content at the high school level, it makes sense to help them pick these skills up as they continue learning instead of stopping and boring them with rote memorization that may feel demeaning and insignificant. Embedding reviews throughout learning is one easy way to support this idea. Just remember, until the underlying concepts and ideas have been overlearned, students' cognitive efforts will be split between lower-level skills and the explicit concept being studied.

REFERENCES

Csikszentmihalyi, M. (1997). *Finding flow*. New York: Basic Books.
Payne, R. K. (2003). *A framework for understanding poverty* (third revised ed.). Highlands, TX: Aha! Process, Inc.
Shepardson, D. P., and Britsch, S. J. (2001). The role of children's journals in elementary school science activities. *Journal of Research in Science Teaching 38*(1): 43–69.

CHAPTER 7

The Downtrodden

March 10

Ivory Hill, after years of notes home, parent phone calls, and low grades, has given up. Though he feels like a disappointment (especially to his single mother), Ivory feels that the only person out there who cares is his girlfriend. Ivory, like other Downtrodden students, doesn't enjoy failure. Yet it seems to be an inescapable cycle. In this chapter, Ivory's constant battle with failure is illustrated.

Five minutes after the start of lunch, teachers slouch into the few remaining chairs in the teachers' lounge. It is Wednesday and the toll of the week shows on the facial expressions around the table.

Mr. Wright sits enjoying the turkey sandwich that his wife prepared that morning, but that quickly changes when Mrs. Boninfante, known as Mrs. B to the students, enters the lounge.

"Good afternoon!" Mrs. B bellows. Mr. Wright tries to hide his grimace as she sits next to him. Mr. Wright adjusts his chair slightly so his back is now effectively to her.

I do not feel like using my lunch hour to discuss her special education students, he thinks. *I'm already grumpy because my wife makes me eat a low-fat diet to lower my blood pressure and cholesterol.*

Mrs. B studies the faces around her and realizes how eclectic the group is today. Ms. Smith busily grades papers that she promised to return two days ago; Mr. Nguyen reads a professional journal while sipping his coffee; and Mrs. Maccabee complains to anyone who will listen about a parent phone call that occurred earlier.

Mrs. B, taking out her thermos of soup, begins to ponder her students. Today she was concerned about Ivory. Since Mr. Wright was not going to begin a conversation, she dove in. "When does the research project for your U.S. history class start?"

"Start?" he states with exasperation. "It's due in two days."

"That's odd," she says. "Ivory hasn't mentioned anything about it. He is in your class, isn't he?"

"Yes," responds Mr. Wright, hoping to not encourage further discussion.

"Well, what has he completed so far?" Mrs. B keeps prodding.

"Nothing."

"Nothing! How come you haven't kept me informed? I continually check the 'Parent Connect' portion of the school website." Her voice is increasing in frustration.

"Well, students are old enough to make their own decisions, and it isn't my job to make sure Ivory has done his assignments. If I wanted to chase after kids and make sure they completed their assignments, Mrs. Boninfante, I would have been an elementary school teacher. My job is to present material. It is the students' job to do something with it." *Besides*, he continues to himself, *one uncompleted assignment means one less to grade.*

"Now if you'll excuse me, I'd like to spend the rest of my lunch period not discussing students."

Mrs. B sits astonished and wonders if he wants all of his students to succeed. After all, isn't that why we are here? Mr. Wright grabs his lunchbox, stands up, and tops off his coffee before heading to class.

Mrs. B knows that not all teachers are as passionate as she is, but how can anyone be so heartless? This is her first time working with Mr. Wright. She heard if you keep the discussion very surface, then he is bearable, but this is too much to handle. Normally, she isn't affected by the negative attitudes of others, but Mr. Wright got to her.

Ms. Smith quietly looks up from her stack of papers, not sure if she should mention Ivory's poor performance in her class as well. With only a few papers left to grade, Ms. Smith decides to join in the discussion.

"Mrs. B, Ivory isn't progressing well on the major English project for my class either. He says he has been working on it in resource but nothing comes back. I sent a note with Ivory to explain the project to you."

Shock covers Mrs. B's face. She asks herself, *What teacher sends a note to another teacher via a student?* Mrs. B knows not to be mad at Kim's first-year teacher mistake, but she feels her blood pressure rising nonetheless. This is Ivory's second time in tenth grade English, and she doesn't want him to fail again.

Ms. Smith nervously continues, "I've called home a few times, but never seem to get anywhere. His mom insists that the school has misdiagnosed her son and that he is really much brighter than the school would like to admit. After all, she insists that she sits and does his homework with him. I just don't know where to go from here."

As she stops speaking, Ms. Smith can see the anguish spreading across Mrs. B's face. Kim hopes that by asking advice it will calm Mrs. B. After all, the last thing Kim needs is to upset her coworkers.

How can teachers effectively interact with parents who had a bad school experience themselves?

Mrs. B ponders how to respond to Ms. Smith. Conversations with Ivory's mother don't typically end in positive ways. Ms. Hill, Ivory's mom, is a single working mother who believes that her child has been misguided by the school system.

For the past ten years, Mrs. Hill has struggled to make ends meet. Moreover, she has been upset with schools ever since Ivory's fifth grade year when the school suggested assessing for learning disabilities. She told the elementary school principal that her son was not stupid and that his teacher just didn't like him, and that's why he was being tested. During Ivory's freshman year, Ms. Hill came to talk with Mrs. B after it was suggested that Ivory might benefit from being in a resource class. Furthermore, it was recommended that Ms. Hill set limits on television, video game, and computer usage at home. Ms. Hill did not have any tolerance for anyone telling her how to raise her son.

> How can teachers balance discussing solutions with parents without being seen as interfering with parenting?

"Ivory never turns in his homework and is generally lazy," Mr. Nguyen chimes in. "I will not invest any more time working with him. Thirteen years of teaching has taught me to spend time and effort on those who care. Besides the kid is seventeen; he has already failed this class. It is time for him to assume some responsibility. The kid can't go through life expecting me to hold his hand."

Mrs. Maccabee pauses her discussion with the other teachers and feels the need to provide her two cents regarding Ivory.

"I also have Ivory. He is my most worthless student. He sleeps and never pays attention on the rare occasion when he is awake. I recommended that he get extra help. If he cares about his future, he would at least try or get some tutoring. I have a family and get paid to work 8:00 to 3:00. Unless I get a big raise, that's what I will continue to do. If he doesn't get it during my class, then it's not my responsibility."

Mrs. B feels her neck get red and quickly responds, "Well, maybe you should consider how to better appeal to students like Ivory. If students feel that you don't care about them, then they aren't going to try."

> How can an effective dialogue be established between special educators and regular teachers to better help all students succeed?

Mrs. Maccabee continues, "My class has a C average, so I must be doing all right. My grades fit the perfect bell curve, which means the hard workers are rewarded. The lazy will continue to be left behind until they put forth the necessary effort to improve. All the administration can ask from me is to reach a majority of the students. Seventy percent of my students are passing with a 60 or above, so I have met the departmental goals." Mrs. Maccabee's tone challenges Mrs. B to continue.

Ms. Smith watches Mrs. B stare in disbelief at Mrs. Maccabee and wonders how one student could have caused such a painful discussion between two experienced teachers. Her college professors warned her to stay away from the teachers' lounge, and now she knows why.

The bell rings, signaling the end of C lunch. The teachers stand up nearly in unison as they venture back to class. Ms. Smith, still shocked by the discussion, turns to Mrs. B, "I would really like to talk to you more about Ivory. I think he just needs some extra guidance. In the future, I guess I should e-mail you instead of relying on Ivory to deliver notes. My prep is third period." Ms. Smith continues toward her classroom as Mrs. B nods, agreeing to a future meeting, then veers toward her own classroom. Ms. Smith tries to clear the lunch discussion from her mind before getting back to her class.

> How can teachers balance building rapport with colleagues with providing the best learning experience for students?

In fifth period, Ms. Smith looks up as the bell chimes to signal the start of class. Ivory, wearing a white long-sleeve T-shirt, jeans, and a Marvin Harrison football jersey, slouches in his seat and stares at the clock as the rest of the students work on their bell work. Today is a "free write." Most students enjoy this activity because they are free to pick their own topic. However, Ms. Smith also realizes that if every day were a free write, it would soon lose its appeal.

As she takes attendance and mentally reviews her lesson plan, she notices that Ivory is not doing the bell work. This continues his pattern of being disengaged. On the rare occasion that he does complete the bell work, she always writes a personalized comment in his binder to encourage such efforts. While waiting for students to finish, she contemplates why Ivory seems so apathetic. Her thoughts are interrupted as she notices that many students are finished writing.

"All right, ladies and gents, it's time to get started. Today we're discussing your autobiographies that are due next Friday. If you have kept up on your work, then you will be fine. However, if you have not been meeting the deadlines, then please talk to me." She looks at Ivory when making these comments, but the eye contact is not returned.

What strategies can be tried to help students who do not complete their work?

As she starts students on some individualized work, she thinks about the personal struggle she has with students like Ivory. As a young dedicated teacher, she lacks confidence in handling the situation. In one respect, these are juniors in high school who should be learning responsibility, and this sometimes means enduring the consequences of poor decisions. In another respect, she does not want to be seen as giving up on the students who struggle. She has struggled with this duality during her first year of teaching.

She never thought that she would continually need to prod students to do their work. Yet she finds herself constantly chasing after students who have not turned in their assignments. With a few minutes left for students to complete their work, she begins checking their papers. She subtly places a *see me* Post-it note on Ivory's paper as she passes his desk.

"Okay, you have thirty seconds to get out a piece of paper and something to write with. I don't want anything else on your desk." Ms. Smith continues, "Now, we are going to explore different ways to tell our personal story through writing. For the next few minutes, brainstorm and then create a timeline of your life. Write birth on the top of your page and high school on the bottom. You have five minutes to brainstorm significant events or defining moments in your life. Once time is up, we will narrow down this list, but right now just write down anything that comes to your mind." Looking around, Ms. Smith sees a sea of blank stares and boredom. Immediately her heart sinks.

After five minutes, she continues, "So what are some things on our lists?" Quickly moving her hands through her hair, she tries to rid the sweat forming around her temples. She has this same reaction every time a lesson starts to fail.

Kevin takes the focus away from her and responds. "I believe that a defining moment in my life was when I went to preschool," he proudly announces. Kevin plays a game at school where he tries to see how many times he can be called on. He loves to be the center of attention.

"Good. Karen, can you tell me why Kevin may have chosen preschool as a defining moment in his life?"

Karen looks up from her paper, still fidgeting with her nail file. "Well, preschool is the first time you are away from your parents for an extended period of time, and it's the beginning of your formal schooling experience," Karen replies.

"Thank you," responds Ms. Smith. She notices Ivory simultaneously gets out a piece of paper, and she is optimistic that he will begin working. She decides to confirm her hunch and asks, "Ivory, can you give me an example?" Looking up from his desk, he stares at her but does not respond. Her optimism quickly turns to feelings of failure. "Can you think of a significant event in your life from birth to high school?" she asks again.

"Nope," Ivory responds.

> What are some other approaches that a teacher can try when students resist sharing?

Seeing the futility in proceeding, Ms. Smith turns to the rest of the class and asks, "Can someone else give me an example?"

"I know. Like, how about when I got my driver's license?" Katie blurts out. "It is important because I am finally free from my parents. Thank God."

Ms. Smith tries to figure out how to respond. She really enjoys Katie as a person, but sometimes Katie blurts out answers. Ms. Smith continues to find effective classroom management challenging.

> How can teachers encourage positive student involvement while suppressing negative, distracting, or dominating students?

"Okay, I am going to give everyone the remaining fifteen minutes of class to compile your list. They are due at the end of class."

Ms. Smith monitors students out of the corner of her eye as she creates a "to do" list for later that day. Hearing a few whispers, she begins walking around the room to make sure students stay on track.

She notices Ivory busily writing, but is it related to the assignment? As Ms. Smith walks over to Ivory's desk, he slips the paper into his pocket. She quickly considers her options and decides to walk past his desk and the situation for the time being.

"Five minutes to finish," exclaims Ms. Smith.

Ivory pulls his note back out and resumes writing as Ms. Smith returns to the front of the class. Smoothing out the page, Ivory reviews his previous scribbles. Upon finishing, he rereads the note to his girlfriend.

Baby girl . . . this day is never going to end. . . . I wish this week was over. I don't want to be bored two more days this week. Ms. Smith tries, but teachers keep tearing me down and say I'm going to fail because I'm lazy. . . . I used to ask questions, but teachers got upset and accused me of not paying attention. I'm done with this crap. I don't know what is worse—school or momma getting on my back. Momma always tryin' to do my homework with me.

She keeps trying to prove that I'm something that I'm not. Teachers never gonna see eye-to-eye with my momma. I am sick of not understanding and always being wrong. Everyone be all up in my face about needin' to be successful after telling me for years that I'm a lazy "waste of potential." Papa and momma didn't finish school, but they pressurin' me to do something they didn't. They say our generation gots no choice. Cousin Jevon only got his GED and he has new clothes and stuff.

Smith just called on me because she knows I'm not paying attention. Why waste her time and mine? It's obvious I don't know the answer so move on instead of makin' me look stupid. I am so sick of teachers always be gettin' on my case. Baby, I better put this note away. I'll talk to you later, baby girl. I love you so much. IH

The daily announcements shock Ivory back into focus. "Teachers please excuse this interruption. . . ." Looking at the clock, Ms. Smith scurries to refocus the last few minutes of class. She hadn't anticipated spending so much time on students sharing the events of their lives. Tuning out the voice of Dean Edwards, Ms. Smith observes the students hurriedly jamming their books, binders, loose papers, and pens into their backpacks. Admitting defeat, she collapses onto her stool at the front of the room. Normally, she reminds students that she determines when class is over—not them—but today she does not have the energy to fight it.

" . . . That's all the afternoon announcements. Thank you for your attention."

Ms. Smith snaps back to reality and suddenly hears herself saying, "All right, ladies and gents, before the announcements started, we were just finishing up this activity. For next time, you need to have your rough drafts completed for peer editing. Are there any . . ." *Beeepppp*!!! Ms. Smith holds her finger up as the bell finishes. Students know to stay put for final comments. "As I was saying, if there are no questions, drop your lists on the podium. Make sure your names are on them. Have a great afternoon."

Students pile out the door and as the last student leaves, she realizes none of the students stayed that she requested, including Ivory. Instead, her Post-it notes remain on desks or litter the floor. She wonders, *How will I ever get through to these kids?*

> How can teachers develop meaningful connections with challenging students like Ivory?

INTERACTING WITH THE DOWNTRODDEN

Few of us have the perseverance of the Edisons and the Dysons (Kelley 2005) to persist even after hundreds of unsuccessful attempts. "I have not failed. I have merely found ten thousand ways that won't work," said Edison as he reflected on his work with numerous inventions. So what makes the Edisons persist when others give up? Part of the answer may reside in our own human psyche, but early successes as a child are critical. If a student begins school lacking many of the expected skills, he or she often enters a downward spiral that reinforces failure instead of building upon prior successes.

Try a small test of your persistence. Take something as simple and familiar as tying a shoe. Only this time try to tie your shoe with one hand. Many will opt out of this exercise because they don't want to look silly struggling with a fundamental skill that we should all have mastered at a younger age. This is not unlike many students in our schools who lack proficiency in basic skills. They continue to operate with one hand obstructed. These students are tired of taking risks only to later be shown that they haven't mastered the essentials. Thus, they fall further behind. This small example makes it a bit easier to understand why some students erect walls to distance themselves from learning opportunities and the teacher.

Fear of failure for the Downtrodden relegates them to a passive role of watching (or ignoring) the success of others. This passiveness is often equated to laziness. I have yet to see a student that was lazy when challenged by things that are attainable and meaningful. The operative word is challenged. Placing students in lower and lower level classes when they fail only serves to continue to lessen the challenge. A downward spiral of greater boredom is the result. Trivial work promotes laziness and boredom. However, be careful because pushing a student beyond their ability will likewise encourage students to shut down. The art of teaching involves scaffolding the level of challenge in attainable ways (Hogan and Pressley 1997; Vygotsky 1978).

The fear of Downtrodden students to engage in school and learning is illustrated by: (1) continual frustration with assignments and activities, (2) giving up quickly and easily, (3) negative comments regarding potential success, and/or (4) an apparent laziness (Marzano, Pickering, and Pollock 2001). On the surface, Downtrodden students like Ivory often downplay the value of assignments with statements such as "This is stupid; I don't understand; this is pointless; I don't get it; I can't do this; why do we have to know this anyway?" Be reminded that most helplessness is temporary; true chronic helplessness is fairly rare (Jensen 1998). Thus, educators have some control in helping reduce the distress felt by their students.

Build on Success

Good teaching is a highly intentional endeavor where the senses are engaged and the participants feel that their uniqueness is celebrated (Gladwell 2000). For teachers to create an interactive, individually unique experience, they must first understand the student. Many schools and districts understand that knowing students necessitates a student-teacher ratio in the range of 80 or 100:1. For settings that demand teachers work with 135+ students per day, knowing our students is still a necessity, so a greater burden is placed on the teacher—often too great a burden. This can result in the teacher also assuming the role of the Downtrodden—they see the goal of success with their students as too much, and they begin to shut down or make excuses. For those who trudge on, there is a high burnout rate.

To aid teachers, an efficient, meaningful system needs to be in place to maximize understanding our students both from an academic and interpersonal perspective. Teachers should know personal issues such as extracurricular interests and job commitments of their students, but they also need to understand the deeper issues such as joys, concerns, passions, and fears. Once interests and past successes are known, learning experiences can be directed in ways to further build success while slowly addressing fears and obstacles. For instance, a student may have a grandparent or parent who has fought in a major conflict or war. Even if the student fears speaking in a group, he or she could record and show an edited video or play an audiotape interview with the family member.

Thus, a personal experience that directly impacts the student and his or her family has become central to learning in a history class. Their experience becomes vital to the learning of everyone and helps improve self-esteem, confidence, and fear of public speaking.

As your class sizes become larger, it becomes critical to create an efficient system to organize student information. One solution dedicates one page in a three-ring binder for each student—alphabetized by class. The top half of the page includes a series of things that the students fill in about themselves during one of the first days of school—including, but also extending beyond, just contact information. The bottom half of the sheet is an area to log reminder notes about new things learned such as a death in the family, a celebration of success, or a conference or phone call to the student (or parent). It is important to be reminded continually of interests and activities of your students. Furthermore, we should take a moment to celebrate birthdays, accomplishments, and successes—either quietly with a note or publicly with the entire class.

Create Learning Opportunities for the Downtrodden that Grow Deficit Skills

Even the most challenging of students possesses an ember of hope, so the goal of the educator becomes identifying strengths and building upon them. Without some intervention, the Downtrodden has little hope for succeeding on major projects such as large term papers in English or creative investigations in science because the components that comprise these projects often remain hidden and elusive. Without first being able to write a coherent paragraph, there is little hope for finding, documenting, and then synthesizing multiple viewpoints into a comparative research paper. So whether breaking a research paper into small, manageable pieces or discussing how to successfully study a scientific question, all students need ways to succeed with all the components that comprise the whole.

When a missing competency is discovered, then a rich opportunity exists to differentiate the instruction. Our goal is to get students to discover how to break learning into pieces and troubleshoot the deficit areas in ways that make sense to them. It is often assumed that by the time students get to high school they have mastered breaking major projects down. Typically, the seeming compromise provided by the teacher to provide a few big chunks or due dates often fails because the gaps are still too large. For instance, teachers often provide a week, give or take a few days, for students to go to the library to conduct research for a term paper. After many students have frittered away a few days, there is a panic in the last day to gather all that is needed. Instead, there should be goals and expectations for students to achieve daily.

Upon entering the library, students should have a sheet of goals that the teacher should be able to check at any point; for instance, "By the end of the period, I will have a minimum of five source cards with notes completed." This is easy for the teacher to spot-check to see if they really know how to document sources and are able to take down meaningful notations to use for their paper. The same reasoning holds true for working on a science project where students may need help in learning to formulate a testable question or gather and analyze data in a meaningful way.

I learned many years ago that ability is meaningless if motivation and desire are lacking. Teachers, schools, and communities are the catalyst for sparking motivation in those who struggle. Roland Barth classifies schools as either learning enriched or learning impoverished (DuFour, DuFour, Eaker, and Karhanek 2004, 38): "I've yet to see a school where the learning curves of the youngsters were off the chart upward while the learning curves of the adults (teachers) are off the chart downward. . . . Teachers and students go hand in hand as learners—or they don't go at all." To personalize this further, is your classroom learning enriched or learning impoverished?

A tendency in our schools is to place the most excited, most skilled, and most capable teachers with the most excited, skilled, and capable students. It is no wonder that in this current tracking system there is such an achievement gap between our students. We first might want to address the achievement gap of our teachers. I think it would be interesting to see what would happen to the achievement gap if you conducted one of the two following experiments: (1) place the students with the lowest motivation with the most skilled and competent teachers and vice versa, or (2) get rid of tracking and have the most skilled and competent teachers be leaders in the dialogue of how to work with all students now that the most capable and the challenged are more equally distributed.

Be reminded that using grades as the motivator is likely to fail for Downtroddens. They have not been successful in this area for years, so using it as the motivator will quickly fail. Make learning the motivator—meaningful, engaging, purposeful learning; fill-in-the-blank worksheets are typically not what is meant here. So how do you teach to the standards and for the test that the district mandates while meaningfully affecting your students? First, until the student cares, the rest will be wasted effort. Often it will take the first six weeks before we can begin to unravel the internal motivators for many of our more challenging students. Immerse content into inquiry experiences whenever possible because content in isolation is merely facts without necessary links to prior knowledge.

We are all fairly similar in some ways. For instance, after repeated difficulty in understanding a concept, topic, or discipline, we tend to tire and begin to tune out things where we are not successful. This lack of attention may be more prevalent with students who have learning disabilities, but it is present in almost all of us. The tendency to withdraw, avoid, or ignore that which seems unattainable is universal, so the goal of the teacher is to find explicit ways to make it attainable. We should not lower our expectations when making learning attainable, but we need to make sure that we start our students on the proper rung of the ladder before encouraging them to climb to the top. The proper starting rung is based on the student's prior knowledge and successes, his or her threshold for challenge, and the essential skills and knowledge that students are to leave with at the end of the year. Remember that despite surface indicators to the contrary, Downtrodden students like Ivory want to experience success. Multiple successes can help create a positive spiraling effect that impacts self-esteem and academic performance.

Encourage Value and Effort

Motivational theorists would argue that both value and expectancy need to occur if students will expend sufficient effort to be successful. Specifically, the effort that students will be willing to invest is dependent upon both the degree to which they expect to be successful on the task and the degree to which they value the rewards and opportunity for performing the task (Brophy 1998). So our goal is to get students to see value in the work, which first and foremost means minimizing trivial work—real or perceived. If the teacher believes that the assignment or investigation has inherent value yet the students do not, then she must do a better job of selling the purpose or relevance to the students.

For students such as the Downtrodden or Overwhelmed, there needs to be a fair system that encourages students to make the necessary effort. Although we cannot or should not base grades on student effort, it is very possible to encourage student effort in ways that promote higher academic achievement. Some credit for effort can be earned when students either maintain high academic performance or continue to improve. To only encourage improvement will get students to sabotage their early grades in a unit so they do not convey understanding too early in the process. However, meaningfully rewarding effort encourages those with lower performance or deficit skills to improve. Credit for completion, filling in worksheets, or participating in a group are unproductive ways to encourage student effort.

REFERENCES

Brophy, J. (1998). *Motivating students to learn*. Boston: McGraw Hill.
DuFour, R., DuFour, R., Eaker, R., and Karhanek, G. (2004). *Whatever it takes: How professional learning communities respond when kids don't learn*. Bloomington, IN: National Educational Service.
Gladwell, M. (2000). *The tipping point: How little things can make a big difference*. New York: Little, Brown.

Hogan, K., and Pressley, M. (eds.). (1997). *Scaffolding student learning: Instructional approaches and issues*. Cambridge, MA: Brookline Books, Inc.

Jensen, E. (1998). *Teaching with the brain in mind*. Alexandria, VA: ASCD.

Kelley, T. (2005). *The ten faces of innovation: IDEO's strategies for beating the devil's advocate and driving creativity throughout your organization*. New York: Doubleday.

Marzano, R. J., Pickering, D. J., and Pollock, J. E. (2001). *Classroom instruction that works: Research-based strategies for increasing student achievement*. Alexandria, VA: ASCD.

Vygotsky, L. (1978). *Mind in society: The development of higher psychological processes*. Cambridge, MA: Harvard University Press.

CHAPTER 8

The Invisible

May 5

John White seems to dissolve in the classroom environment. He follows the teacher's directions, but rarely raises his hand, inquires about his grade, or talks with the teacher during class. Similar to other Invisible students, John's presence in the classroom is rarely felt. When he is absent, he is not missed, and he continues to slip further through the "cracks" of the education system. In this chapter, we see the Invisible surface when a low grade demands the attention be focused on him.

Mrs. Maccabee replaces the phone receiver to its hook and slowly releases a long, deep sigh. She just listened to a parent message from the mother of one of her students, John White.

"Hello, Mrs. Maccabee. This is Sandy White calling about my son, John White, whom you have in your seventh-hour geometry class. I'm calling because I see that John has a D in your class. I am wondering why I was not contacted earlier in the semester due to his low grade. I was under the impression that teachers are supposed to contact parents when a child is in danger of failing a class and losing credit for the semester. Please call me after school today to discuss the matter. I can be reached anytime after 3:00 at 555-2727. Thanks."

Mrs. Maccabee sighs again. Three more weeks until the end of the school year, and Mrs. White wants to talk *now*? Mrs. Maccabee is not against talking with parents. She understands the importance of fostering healthy parent-teacher relationships and sees this communication as part of her responsibility. As an overinvolved parent herself, she has many times assumed the role of the mother on the other end of the receiver. But discussing credit and grades three weeks before the semester ends? Why not earlier in the term?

Mrs. Maccabee looks at her thin, red grade book. It provides a back-up in case the computer fails or in case she is at home and does not have access to the electronic grade book. Though she knows electronic grade books are reliable, she still resists fully transitioning from paper to all electronic.

Mrs. Maccabee's policy states that she will contact parents if their son or daughter has a D or F in her class. Mrs. Maccabee stays late at school on Tuesday evenings. Dedicating one evening to work provides a concentrated time to update the grade book and make most all the necessary parent contacts for the week. She also takes care of extra grading and lesson planning on those late Tuesday nights.

Mrs. Maccabee is nearly positive that she already called and talked with Sandy White about John's grade in math. However, to be on the safe side, she checks her parent contact binder. In her binder, she logs all her parent phone calls with the date, time, whom she contacted, the reason for the contact, and the resolution. Mrs. Maccabee is very thorough with her binder. Tracking this information in such a detailed manner is a way for Mrs. Maccabee to protect herself.

How do teachers ensure accurate, consistent parent contact? What is an effective method for tracking parent/student interactions?

Mrs. Maccabee's fingers quickly find the *W* section of the binder— Way . . . Warren . . . White. There it is. It is blank. What?! Mrs. Maccabee wonders how this error happened. At the front of the parent contact binder, there is a sheet with the name of every student whose parents she has contacted regarding grades, and Mrs. Maccabee feels that John's name can surely be found on the list. She flips to the front and scans the list. Yes, there it is. The problem, however, is that Mrs. Maccabee has forgotten to contact the parents of the last three students on the list—White, Yates, and Youngblood. It is now clear why John's parents never received a call. This realization does not erase the mistake, but at least she knows what happened.

How does a teacher correct a mistake when it involves a parent or student?

Needing to receive assurance from a coworker, Mrs. Maccabee wanders down the hall to Mr. Nguyen's classroom.

"Tony, do you have a minute?" Mrs. Maccabee asks as she briskly walks into his room.

"Sure. What's going on?" Mr. Nguyen replies.

"John White. You have him in class, don't you? What grade does he have for you?"

Mr. Nguyen's eyes scan the names on the electronic grade book, pausing on John White.

Mr. Nguyen states inquisitively, "John has a C. Why do you ask?"

With a frustrated smile, Mrs. Maccabee replies, "John's mom called me this morning and wants me to call her after school today because John has a low D in my class. And checking my parent call book, I discovered that I forgot to call her about John's grade. I feel awful that I didn't contact her, but I also don't understand what she expects to come from a telephone call when we are only three weeks shy of the end of the year."

Mr. Nguyen replies, "Good luck with that call. I talked with Sandy White a couple of weeks ago about John and his grade, and let's just say she's not the easiest to talk to. She takes charge of the conversation so much that you can barely get in a word. When I got off the phone with her, I felt that she hadn't heard me at all, and we were back to where we had started before the call. In her eyes, John can do no wrong."

"Oh, no," Mrs. Maccabee groans. "That's just what I need at the end of an already long week."

"Well, trust me, it's better to take care of the problem today instead of leaving it up to her to track you down. Besides, we have a faculty meeting at 3:30 p.m. today—a sure way to keep your conversation short."

Mrs. Maccabee slowly smiles. "Good point, Tony. I'll do just that. Thanks for the help!"

How can teachers who share the same students effectively work together to gain a better understanding of their students?

Skateboards. Skateboarding. Those two things fill John's mind as he sits in the lunchroom with two of his friends, Randy and Jeff. The only mental activity that lunch requires each day is whether to get the special or go through the à la carte line. John decides on the special—the school's mystery meat, corn, peaches, and pudding.

"Earth to John," Randy states while giving John a poke in the shoulder. "We're going to the new skate park after school today. Are you in?"

"Yeah, man," John states. "I'm in." After he thinks about it for a second, though, John realizes that he has a huge Spanish test the next day. *Oh well, it doesn't matter*, John thinks. What's the point of learning regular and irregular verbs? It is not like he is planning to visit Spain anytime soon.

John has more important things than Spanish on his mind. As he tentatively takes another bite of the meat on his tray, he thinks about the skate park. It just officially opened three days ago. Three ramps, five rails, and smooth pavement everywhere the eye can see—a skateboarder's dream come true. No more grocery store managers chasing him away from their parking lots. No more assistant principals yelling at him for skating on the sidewalks outside of the school. Plus, the park is only five minutes from his house. *What a great start to the summer*, he thinks.

John's thoughts are interrupted by the bell. Science then geometry then skateboarding—John cannot wait. . . .

Mrs. Maccabee stands in the hall watching students throw their books into their already overflowing lockers, exchanging them for the final round of books needed for the day. She shouts at a student to put away his iPod; tells two students that, yes, they have time to get a drink from the water fountain but they better hurry; and half-listens to Mr. Wright as he talks about highlights from *SportsCenter* last night.

Detecting a bit of frustration on the part of Mrs. Maccabee, Mr. Wright questions, "What's gotten under your skin, Susan?"

"It's not a what, it's a who," Mrs. Maccabee replies. "I need to call Sandy White, John White's mom, after school today, and she is not too happy that I haven't called her sooner about her son's poor academic performance."

As if on cue, John passes Mrs. Maccabee on his way into her class but not before shooting her a look of contempt, as if saying, "I can't believe I have to waste my time in your class again."

"What is *that* look for?" Mr. Wright asks after John passes and then enters the classroom.

"That's John White. It's his mother that I will be talking with this afternoon."

"Hum . . . puny little kid. Couldn't play tennis even if he wanted to!" Mr. Wright reassures Mrs. Maccabee. He spits out the word *tennis* as if he barely considers the game a sport—let alone a respectable one.

The bell rings, signaling the beginning of the seventh and final period. Mrs. Maccabee walks into the room and closes the door behind her, ensuring the silence in the room would remain. Her students rarely work on the daily warm-up activity unless prodded to do so, but today is different—all students attempt to solve the triangle and rhombus proof. Mrs. Maccabee sternly talked to them about their behavior yesterday. She included a couple of empty threats about calling home, so she knew that the class would behave reasonably well for at least a day or two.

The period passes quickly. Mrs. Maccabee leads them through the warm-up then gives a short quiz. With the last twenty minutes of class, she reviews yesterday's concepts. As the class works on solving the proofs, Mrs. Maccabee calls on students to share their solutions with the rest of the class. Particularly attuned to John White, she notices that he never raises his hand during the period. Not once does he try to talk out of turn or leave his seat without permission. He just sits there, with his pencil in his hand and his eyes transfixed to his paper as if to say, "Don't call on me. Pretend I'm not here!"

No wonder I don't notice when he's absent, Mrs. Maccabee thinks to herself. *I barely recognize when he is here because he's so withdrawn and quiet.*

Meanwhile, John thinks, *I can't wait until school is over. I am ready to go home and try out my new board at the park.* John really does not see the point of participating in school. From his point of view, whether he talks or doesn't talk does not really seem to matter. Either way he still has to do the homework. Furthermore, his grade is based on what he turns in and not what he says in class.

What percentage of a student's grade, if any, should be determined by class participation? What does full participation look like?

Besides, John has always been shy around large groups of people. Ever since stuttering became a problem in third grade, he has been afraid to speak. Even though he no longer stutters, he never voluntarily talks in front of the twenty-five-plus classmates that share each class with him. Luckily, his parents are very understanding. They usually do most of the talking for him—even when others call upon him to reply. His mother understands that her *baby* is only a sophomore and still needs assistance conquering his fear of public speaking.

"John, what measurement do you have for the third angle?" Mrs. Maccabee asks.

John panics a bit, scans his paper, and then slowly starts to mumble the correct answer. His work and answer are accurate, but he dislikes speaking in front of his classmates. Mrs. Maccabee asks him to speak up a bit because she cannot hear him. Luckily, though, John is saved by the bell.

The students quickly grab their strewn papers and books and race out the door as if they are animals and can smell the freedom that the hallways provide. Mrs. Maccabee calls after them, "Don't forget about your homework—page 551, numbers 1–40, evens only!"

After all the students leave, Mrs. Maccabee sits at her desk and quickly scans her grade book. She sighs. She has to return Sandy White's call, use the restroom, get a snack, and be at the faculty meeting in twenty-seven minutes. As she dials the number, she mentally compiles a list of what she intends to say.

"Hello. You've reached the voicemail of Sandy White. I am unable to take your call right now . . ."

Mrs. Maccabee waits until the end of the message and then begins. "Hi, Mrs. White. This is Susan Maccabee from Roosevelt High returning your call about John's geometry grade. John has a low D in my class due to his scores on the last two tests as well as two incomplete homework assignments. John also rarely participates in class. For example, today I only heard from him once and only because I called upon him to give his answer. If you have any questions or further concerns, please feel free to call me. Thanks. Have a good afternoon."

Mrs. Maccabee hangs up and slowly breathes out a sigh of relief. She records the details of the phone call in her parent calls' binder, and then realizes that she forgot to mention ways that John can improve his grade between now and the end of the term. Oh well, she is not about to call again. With a few extra minutes to spare, Mrs. Maccabee quickly enters the grades on the quiz for her two earlier classes—one less thing that she will need to do this weekend. There's always something to do. . . .

INTERACTING WITH THE INVISIBLE

Leaving John White, the Invisible, until the end of the apathy discussion only seems appropriate. If we take a few minutes to scan our class rosters, it quickly becomes evident that there are many—far too many—students that we vaguely know or understand beyond the grades that we enter in the grade book. The personalities and ability levels of these students vary considerably, yet the commonality that binds them as a group is the ability for them to blend into the social fabric and largely go unrecognized in our classrooms in any significant way. In a very real sense, the Invisible epitomizes the norm. When one becomes too much an average of the whole, there does not seem to be anything left that merits recognition.

Compare the Invisible to some of the other forms of apathy. The Rebel desires some of the Invisible's anonymity but seems to repeatedly stand out in negative ways. The Socialite thrives on commanding attention and leading the interpersonal venue. Additionally, many of the other highlighted archetypes receive teacher attention for a myriad of reasons, but the appearance, behavior, and performance of the Invisible become muted by the surrounding interactions. So what strategies may be helpful to guide teachers when working with Invisibles such as John White?

Intentionally Interact with All Students

First, the point is not to encourage students to become someone that they are not. Rather, we, as teachers, need to adjust our perceptual focus to make sure that all students are *seen* in ways that are appropriate for them. Let's consider the focus of most books that are available to assist and guide practitioners in the classroom. Typical topics include working with the geniuses in our classrooms, strategies for special needs students, succeeding with English as second language students, and motivating failing students. The common theme of these books is how to challenge the high flyers and how to get the lower achievers to succeed.

I have yet to run across a book that focuses on how to teach to the middle of the pack, how to excel with those who pass but do not value school, or more poignant still, how to teach to the average Joe. The fact is that no one wants to pick up such a book—there is no flash or intrigue, even though this book represents a good portion of the student body at most American high schools. Maybe the point is to find better ways (and time) to work with the quietest cog in the machine—one that is not screaming, demanding, or overly excited, and that should be reason enough.

One way to intentionally refocus our attention so that all students become central to our focus is to give extra attention to three students in each class each day. An easy way to remember to do this is to use the index cards that many teachers have students fill out at the beginning of the school year. Begin with the three students on the top of the stack and familiarize yourself with their interests, abilities, goals, and concerns. Note these students on a Post-it that you carry with you throughout the day. This arrangement provides a constant reminder to systematically interact and engage with all students on a regular basis. With each ensuing day, rotate the cards to the back of the pile, thus revealing three new students that you will focus extra attention toward before, during, or at the end of class.

For a class of thirty, this means that at least every other week or four to five times throughout each quarter, you will intentionally communicate in more significant ways with each student in each class. The method that you choose to engage with these students does not have to be complicated. It may be as simple as saying a few words to them at the door as they enter class or pausing at their desk a little longer during an assignment to check and see how things are going. But it can also be more significant and complex if you choose as well. It might mean that you spend a little extra time writing comments in their science journals or essays in an effort to make a stronger connection. You will quickly learn what is comfortable for each student.

Encourage Intrinsic Motivation Whenever Appropriate

The goal is not to seek deep lifelong personal relationships with all our students. For one thing, time is lacking to achieve this goal—particularly when working with one hundred or more students. Furthermore, you will naturally connect better with some students than others—this connection occurs partly because of our individual personalities. However, we do have a responsibility to foster the development of *all* our students as far as we possibly can during a given academic year. So what can be done?

Building positive rapport has repeatedly surfaced in the previous discussions as a critical component of succeeding with at-risk or apathetic students, so the point will not be belabored here again. Yet, another issue is worth considering—the role of intrinsic and extrinsic motivation in our classroom structure. Research is divided regarding implementation of instruction that employs intrinsic or extrinsic motivation, and, like many things in life, being too extreme in anything is fraught with problems.

Some contend that providing extrinsic incentives (rewards for good performance) is merited to get low-performing students to care in the first place. Constantly providing a carrot for performance will soon backfire, resulting in students only performing if they see the reward. For Overachievers, this reward is the grade or points that are earned, but for others it may be for the pizza party or candy bar if they succeed. Alfie Kohn (1993; 1999) represents the other view and denounces the use of extrinsic motivators. While the idealism is wonderful, Kohn's position seems too radical in the other direction for most teachers to feasibly attain within the confines of their current system. Since extreme problems exist at either end of the continuum, what are sensible and logical options for teachers as they work within their current framework?

Jere Brophy (1998) is one who endorses a more relativistic position that claims there are times that warrant using extrinsic incentives such as candy, bonus points, or other bribes, but there are also times when intrinsic incentives (e.g., seeing the enjoyment of learning and learning for the sake of learning) are merited. At times it would be nice to be able to rewind the clock, but the fact is that by the time students reach high school, they have been barraged by a constant peppering of extrinsic reward structures. Currently our society operates by a system that says that the person who accumulates the most money, power, or fame wins. As teachers, we need to be aware and honest regarding the state in which our students enter our classrooms.

Kohn, Brophy, and most all motivational theorists understand that for lifelong learning to occur, students need to become intrinsically motivated. The question becomes where and how. Just as we must scaffold the learning experiences that we lead in our classrooms, we must also scaffold the way that incentive structures are transformed from predominantly extrinsic to more intrinsic. To just walk in and support an intrinsic-only philosophy will be too foreign for students to grasp, so making explicit steps to achieve this transformation is critical. Moreover, if the concept is one of the most important ideas that frame your class, then you should work toward encouraging intrinsic motivation to learn. Wiggins and McTighe (1998) call these critical learning components that frame our courses' enduring ideas.

We can encourage and support intrinsic motivation of these critical ideas by providing substantive, thought-provoking hooks. Specifically, which class would you rather attend? Which would actively engage you? The one whose whiteboard reads "What would your life be like if your freedom of speech was limited (e.g., rap music was banned, newspapers written solely by the government)"? Or the board that reads "First Amendment"? Providing engaging ideas that spark curiosity is something that we can do on a regular basis. Students need to see a reason to care before intrinsic motivation becomes possible.

So when are extrinsic motivators appropriate? Anything that is memorized solely to help reduce the cognitive load later is a good candidate. There is nothing really exciting about learning the multiplication tables or memorizing the symbols for the most commonly used elements. Furthermore, we learn them so we can later apply them to more enduring ideas. This distinction of being a means to an end provides a solid reason to encourage learning through extrinsic motivation. The goal is to get students to proficiency quickly and effectively for rote learning, so whatever means encourages students to do so seem fair game. While the goal is to build intrinsic value in learning, there are times when learning is not alluring, fun, or exciting. During those times, provide the encouragement for students to master the ideas so that the more intriguing lifelong learning pieces can become the focus.

REFERENCES

Brophy, J. (1998). *Motivating students to learn*. Boston: McGraw-Hill.

Kohn, A. (1993). *Punished by rewards: The trouble with gold stars, incentive plans, As, praise, and other bribes*. Boston: Houghton Mifflin.

————. (1999). *The schools our children deserve: Moving beyond the traditional classrooms and "tougher standards."* Boston: Houghton Mifflin.

Wiggins, G., and McTighe, J. (1998). *Understanding by design*. Alexandria, VA: ASCD.

CHAPTER 9

Conclusion

As teachers we seek to succeed with each student that enters our classroom. This desire to affect the minds and lives of our students in positive ways is where we start. The ideals that we stand for quickly become challenged as reality enters the equation. By the time pre-service teachers finish their student-teaching experience, they see a reality where high school students largely lack a thirst for knowledge or a passion to learn in any of the core disciplines (mathematics, science, English, and social studies). So the question becomes what we can do to bridge the chasm between our romanticized idealisms and the often apathetic reality that confronts us in our classrooms.

This discussion began with several questions that most teachers, neophyte or experienced, must confront before maximal success can be attained with all students. Some of these questions included:

- Is the expectation that *all* students can and will learn reasonable and possible, or is it too idealistic?
- Do teachers expect failure from some students?
- How do you work with students who *appear* lazy or unmotivated?
- How far should a teacher go to provide students with engaging, meaningful learning opportunities?
- How do you set high expectations and hold students accountable when they don't want to take any responsibility?

These are all complex issues where a single solution is not likely. Any attempt to find one only trivializes the complex nature of the challenges before us. Therefore, the numerous strategies and questions contained within this book are meant to provide a starting point to begin exploring the complex world of teaching without attempting to provide a magic bullet. When we progress beyond panaceas and our own fear, then we are able to explore, question, and most importantly embark on solutions together as a coherent team.

In our quest for a solution to the apathy that plagues our schools, we must realize that our students' lives are often difficult and filled with troubles that sometimes extend beyond our current realm of understanding or empathy. Yet we are expected, in the short time that we have with them, to assist each student to learn and grow in significant ways. This goal is undoubtedly challenging but still attainable. Specifically, this goal necessitates that we guide each student to a minimum level of competency.

Disagreements exist about what this minimum competency looks like, but it seems clear that any definition should provide an attainable challenge for the academically challenged as well as those who are gifted. This means that if a student enters ninth grade with fourth-grade abilities in mathematics, minimum competency should include advancing through *several* of the deficit grade levels over the course of the year. Part of the plan should include projecting when the student will be performing at grade-level competency and communicating this to both the parents and student.

Likewise, for a ninth grade student who enters with senior-level mathematics skills and abilities, he or she should have to demonstrate success at the level of a college freshman at least in mathematics. Collectively, finding appropriate ways to challenge both gifted and struggling students is a Jeffersonian idea that requires an educational system that provides a balance of true, genuine learning opportunities while realizing that all will not strive to the same level. However, a significant, attainable minimum should be set for all students.

Having an action plan in mind to challenge all students is imperative, but a significant portion of success requires that we first find ways to erode the ever-present world of apathy that confronts us. The eight archetypes explored illustrate many of the unique manifestations of apathy in schools today. The various archetypes can be summarized as follows:

- The Rebel uses anger as a defense mechanism to hide deficit skills and knowledge.
- The Socialite emphasizes the interpersonal in an effort to combat the perceived lack of relevance in the academic portion of school.
- The Misfit, whether pushed aside or choosing to withdraw, is largely socially inept.
- The Overachiever represents the skillful master of playing the game of school, where grades and rewards obscure sincere efforts to learn.
- The Player finds motivation only in nonacademic things and thus constantly struggles in classroom settings.
- The Overwhelmed attempts to see all the pieces at once, which leads to abundant stress and undue frustration.
- The Downtrodden becomes resigned to lack of success after experiencing years of failure in the current educational system.
- The Invisible truly embodies the norm so much that they become transparent to others and lack a defined identity.

The prevalence or combination of each archetype will be influenced by numerous factors that include cultural and socioeconomic differences. Encouragement can be found in knowing the great influence that teachers can have on students—regardless of the challenges that exist when they enter our classrooms. Specifically, efforts to improve the relational quality between the teacher and students and among students are critical steps for improving the interactions with all archetypes. Furthermore, the environment that we create to encourage communication and learning is vital if some of the defensive walls are to be removed.

What happens in the lives of our students before they arrive in our classes is beyond our control, but how we help them process the past, confront the present, and strive toward the future is within our power to affect. In the process of helping students process the past, we must help them advance developmentally, academically, and socially. Developmentally, we can assist as students transition from a very structured, nurturing environment to one where they ultimately need to strive to be independent, lifelong learners. Academically, we must learn to build from the prior knowledge of our students as they seek to transfer prior learning to new and more complex ideas. And, socially, our students need to see how the interpersonal world can be used to communicate in effective and appropriate ways.

As we wrestle with the various manifestations of apathy in our classrooms, it becomes apparent that the challenge is not just what we can *do to* them. Rather, the challenge becomes how we can grow together in the pursuit of success. This distinction is significant because our tendency is to *do things to* students. Specifically, our default modus operandi is to lecture to students instead of engaging them in learning. Granted, this default is present because that is largely what was done to us and modeled for us as we went to school. To break from such an ingrained paradigm likely will require more than an overnight epiphany. In fact, most have had the epiphany long ago only to have it squashed when reality confronted their current skills in working with students who have been steeped in apathy many years by the time they reach high school.

A paradigmatic shift can occur in many ways. Several stages occur as one transitions from the old system to the new paradigm and may include the following: (1) clearly acknowledge the problem, (2) believe that you have a role in the solution (quit the blame game) and be specific as to what that role is, (3) engage others in the effort, (4) realize that some will be resistant to embarking on the proposed journey, (5) accept where your students begin and seek success from that point, (6) set high standards but be realistic in your ability to impart change, (7) realize overcompensation is common when undergoing a paradigm shift, and (8) find ways to reinvigorate your passion. A few points of clarification are necessary.

First, know that we are all at different points in our development and philosophical beliefs as teachers, so do not become discouraged if others are not as excited about change and improvement as you are. When trying something new, there usually is an overcompensation that initially occurs. For instance, if you explicitly seek to identify and draw out the Invisibles in your class, you will likely do this at the expense of giving equal time to others. Eventually, stability will be reached where a balance of energy and time is achieved with all students.

To conclude, sometimes we just need to know that we are not alone. The need to engage in a corporate discussion regarding the problem of apathy cannot be emphasized enough. The statistics are manipulated in many different ways, but the bottom line is that approximately one in three freshmen entering school in America does not make it to graduation in a timely manner. This number is as high as one in two in some states such as South Carolina. Yes, some pick up GEDs along the way, but for the rest, we as a society have failed them. The success rate in higher education is even more abysmal.

The personal expense to us as educators to change the current system requires giving a little more time and effort while at times being willing to put our pride aside. Simply put, if each teacher gets three or four students back on track in ways that build confidence and academic success, there would be millions fewer problems to challenge us as educators at the end of the year. The extended implications include fewer imprisoned, impoverished, and downtrodden youth—isn't that worth the effort?

Finally, currently we are in a lose-lose situation where many of our students are disengaged in the learning process, and we become frustrated or apathetic ourselves because our efforts have not helped them succeed. The status switches to a win-win when students begin to realize fully their potential, and we see value in our efforts to guide learning. Educators, administrators, legislators, and even parents can try to deny the realities, but this will only serve to perpetuate the achievement gap between the haves and the have-nots; the franchised and the disenfranchised; the affluent and the poor; the white and the black. We can no longer afford to deny the reality before us, particularly when good solutions exist to improve the current system. Learning and teaching are a journey that students and teachers can undertake in unison or in opposition. When in harmony, the potential is unlimited.

About the Authors

JEFF C. MARSHALL

Jeff Marshall began his career by quickly ascending the corporate ladder. He became vice president of a large home-building corporation, where he soon realized that he desired more. In 1991, he united his passions for working with youth and studying science and began his teaching career. During the next seventeen years, the journey has taken him on environmental studies explorations to the rainforests of Costa Rica and to the World Solar Rally in Japan to race a solar vehicle built by his students. His innovations in working with at-risk students earned the Presidential Award for Excellence in Mathematics and Science Teaching.

Currently, Dr. Marshall is assistant professor at the Moore School of Education at Clemson University, where he works with pre-service middle and high school science teacher preparation and with improving in-service teacher quality. In addition to addressing student apathy, his work on integrating mathematics and science education and promoting inquiry-based teaching practices has appeared in numerous practitioner and research journals.

DINA BAILEY

At an early age, Dina Bailey developed a passion for helping others. She gives credit to her mother, Starlee Bailey, an educator in the public school system, for her determination to make a difference in the lives of adolescents. Dina graduated from Butler University in 2004, with a degree in middle/secondary education, English. Her teaching experience includes positions in urban high schools in both Indianapolis and Cincinnati. She earned a master's degree in anthropology of development and social transformation at the University of Sussex in Brighton, England. Currently, Dina works at the National Underground Railroad Freedom Center in Cincinnati, Ohio, as a curator. No matter what avenue she pursues, Dina is dedicated to the positive fulfillment of world citizenship through engagement and education.

BRIAN DUNN

Brian Dunn holds a BA in English and 5–12 Certification from Butler University and an MFA in creative writing from Purdue University. Brian has taught both creative writing and composition at Purdue, winning multiple awards. Brian has worked with all types of students, from three-year-olds diagnosed with autistic spectrum disorders to grandmothers returning to college for the joy of learning. The diversity of Brian's experience has allowed him to develop a more flexible and effective classroom—one where students can adapt the course to their own learning styles and talents.

EMILY LASZEWSKI

Chosen as an Eli Lilly Community Endowment scholar, Emily Laszewski attended Butler University in Indianapolis, Indiana. While attending Butler University, Emily was recognized as a Butler University Designated Scholar in Education and was involved with Kappa Delta Pi, the Student Education Association, and Butler University's Writers' Studio. She has been a classroom teacher since graduating in 2004. Currently, Emily serves on her school's Safe School Committee, spearheads an English Academic Superbowl team, and works alongside parents to ensure the success of all her students.

ABIGAIL PARKER-KINDELSPERGER

Abigail Parker-Kindelsperger began working with youth at age fourteen in capacities that include Boys and Girls Club staff member, tutor, and athletic coach. She graduated summa cum laude from Butler University in 2005 with degrees in middle/secondary education and English. For her honors thesis, Abigail studied the representation of gender roles in the literature curriculum of India, Australia, and Canada. After graduation, Abigail taught at a public high school in Indianapolis, Indiana, and a private school for students with learning disabilities in New York. Currently Abigail attends the Ohio State University as a graduate student in the School of Teaching and Learning, where she also supervises student teachers as a graduate associate. Abigail's passions for learning, youth, and literature inspire all of her endeavors.

ALICIA SMITH-NONEMAN

Alicia Smith-Noneman is a 2004 cum laude graduate from Butler University, where she was awarded the Joseph M. Nygard Community and University Service Award and the Top 100 Outstanding Student Award. In addition, Alicia's membership in several academic honoraries includes Phi Eta Sigma, Alpha Lambda Delta, Blue Key, National Society of Collegiate Scholars, Kappa Delta Pi, and Mortar Board. After graduating with a BS in middle/secondary education, Alicia took a position at Carmel High School in Carmel, Indiana, where she teaches U.S. history, U.S. government, and advanced placement comparative politics. While at Carmel, she has continued to further her education by pursuing her master's in political science and receiving training in English-language learning. Alicia's pursuit of lifelong learning has taken her on ventures to Europe and Washington, DC, with her students.